COMING TO TERMS

Roberta Israeloff teaches writing at Hunter College and New York University. She was cited as an outstanding writer in *The Pushcart Prize IV: The Best of the Small Presses*, 1979–80, and her stories have also appeared in *North American Review* and *Pig Iron*. She lives in New York City with her husband and son.

COMING
to
TERMS

Roberta Israeloff

PENGUIN BOOKS

PENGUIN BOOKS
Viking Penguin Inc., 40 West 23rd Street,
New York, New York 10010, U.S.A.
Penguin Books Ltd, Harmondsworth, Middlesex, England
Penguin Books Australia Ltd, Ringwood, Victoria, Australia
Penguin Books Canada Limited, 2801 John Street,
Markham, Ontario, Canada L3R 1B4
Penguin Books (N.Z.) Ltd, 182–190 Wairau Road,
Auckland 10, New Zealand

First published in the United States of America by
Alfred A. Knopf Inc. 1984
Published in Penguin Books 1985

LIBRARY OF CONGRESS CATALOGING IN PUBLICATION DATA
Israeloff, Roberta, 1952–
Coming to terms.
1. Pregnancy—Psychological aspects.   2. Pregnant
women—United States—Biography.   3. Mother and child.
4. Infants—Care and hygiene—Psychological aspects.
5. Mothers—United States—Biography.   I. Title.
[RG525.I78   1985]   155.6′463   85-9439
ISBN 0 14 00.8342 1

Portions of this work were originally
published in *Glamour* and *Self* magazines.

Printed in the United States of America by
R. R. Donnelley & Sons Company, Harrisonburg, Virginia
Set in Janson

For Benjamin

Acknowledgments

*I'd like to thank
Benjamin's grandparents,
Jack and Rae, and Marvin and Phyllis,
for unflagging support and hours of expert babysitting
without which this book could not have been finished.
And to Ben's father,
my loving helpmeet,
David,
a special thanks.*

CONTENTS

1

Wading In

WHEN WE WERE growing up, my friends and I rarely talked about having children. I think most of us assumed we would but in a future we couldn't describe and certainly didn't believe would ever arrive. I alone was going to remain childless, not out of desire but by design. Whatever mechanical or chemical snag that had always caused my menstrual periods to show up unannounced at odd moments, like peripatetic friends, was also going to preclude my conceiving. While nearly every other female acquaintance underwent at least one abortion, I, the only one who admitted to wanting children, tried on words like "barren" and mustered up a healthy store of inadequacy. I was either exceptionally assiduous about birth control or sterile. Dramatically, I assumed the second.

This freed me to anticipate my childlessness as the crowning irony of my life and long for children with an urgency that shocked me. I had never thought of myself as particularly maternal; I had never enjoyed playing house or babysitting, and I certainly didn't care for my younger sister during her early years. In fact, her arrival was so traumatic that I successfully obliterated the entire episode from my mind, beginning with my mother's pregnancy. Only one memory is perfectly clear. Sandwiched between my mother and nurse in the back seat of the car driving home from the hospital, I waited eagerly to hold my baby sister. But once she was in my arms, her scowl blossomed into ear-splitting wails and I wanted to chuck her. My mother claims she found me beating up

3

the baby in her crib, but this I don't remember. I do recall throwing rocks at passing cars and hitting younger kids during playtime. Eventually, it must have dawned on me that hating babies wasn't especially becoming. I'd do better to try to figure out a way of loving them.

The gynecologist I consulted in college—the first time in stirrups without my mother watching—a kindly, middle-aged Italian doctor with a barely understandable accent, was far more concerned about my menses than hypothetical children. He sent me home with a basal thermometer which I was to pop in my mouth, if possible, a moment before awakening; if not, before opening my second eye—and a temperature chart on which to record each day's reading. Above the space allotted each day was a box for indicating that coitus had occurred, and squares to darken during menstruation. Other events which might upset my thermostat—fevers, stomach disorders, insomnia—were also to be noted.

When I returned months later with my chart, the doctor studied it long enough to count every check mark. Two spontaneous ovulations had taken place, proving that my body worked, if a bit capriciously. "Relax," he said. "Get married, have a baby, then you'll be regular." I tried to explain that I cared about regularity only to the extent that it impinged on my ability to become pregnant. "You'll get pregnant," he said. "Relax. Get married."

So many of his prescriptions included such nonmedical advice that most of my friends eventually stopped seeing him. Only to me were his words comforting. It seemed beyond his understanding that I might be sterile, and so I remained his patient for many years, returning for semi-annual doses of professional optimism.

During his adolescence, David also had worried about his ability to have children, fearing that his sperm was the wrong color—too grayish. This was only one of the many coincidences bespeaking a deeper rapport which we discovered during our long, rambling walks. Actually, we spent much of what became our courtship as pedestrians, talking about our neuroses, pasts, fears, aspirations. Neither one of us ever proposed; instead we fantasized aloud and watched the fantasies dovetail. "I can see our house," he said one day. We were walking in Central Park; it was early spring. "You'll have your study and a sewing room. We'll have a piano. I'll have a barn to convert into a music studio."

"And a basketball hoop for the kids," I said.

"They'll have their separate wing of the house," he added.

"And plenty of land all around, so we can sleep out on summer nights." Children inhabited both our future visions—children practicing piano, swinging baseball bats, learning harmonies, watching late night movies with us, climbing into bed with us on Sunday mornings.

What we were really doing was acknowledging another compatibility—we were both waders. Divers at the sight of a beach hurl themselves down the stretch of sand and thrust themselves into the oncoming wave. We stand at the water's edge with only our big toes in the water. "It's very cold," we tell each other. After a few minutes, we wet our ankles. Next we unfold our arms and splash water on our faces and chests, like old people. Those who dove in are already heading out, shaking water off their limbs like dogs. We wait for a cloud to move away from the sun. Finally we turn around and, with our backs to the surf and our eyes fastened on the sand, we bend our knees imperceptibly as if sinking into an easy chair, and take the shock of water with eyes closed, sitting down.

Having successfully and painlessly waded into marriage, we assumed that we would eventually find ourselves having babies. Positing children at some mythic "right time" which would identify itself as such, we took a trip to Europe, worked hard, saved money. Three years passed. We felt emotionally mature, yet not a whit closer to forswearing time together. Our financial situation was deplorable but unlikely to improve for several years, at which time biology might be against us. Maybe there was no right time. Maybe this was the right time and we didn't know it. Maybe there was no way for us to wade into this decision.

I had learned the facts of life in Bayside, Queens, on the corner of Bell Boulevard and 75th Avenue, waiting for the red light to change on the way home for lunch. I was eleven years old, in sixth grade. The information, offered in a casual way, stunned me, but I knew enough to keep calm. Even though the source was my best friend —a reliable girl—it was quite literally "street knowledge" and I, who had been sure that quite a different system obtained, needed confirmation.

My mother was in the kitchen cleaning chickens. A tuna sandwich awaited me; I pushed it away. Choosing a perfect segue, I began: "That book I just finished reading, *Cheaper by the Dozen;* that couple decided on their wedding night to have twelve kids. I thought you had no say in the matter."

She washed her hands, sat down, and thinking that she had to explain rather than validate, used up a lot of time and words. Most of what she said I understood only in a general way, but it was enough to corroborate my friend's version. I'm sure she was relieved when it was over, especially since I took it so well, unable to muster up a suitable show of disgust after my initial wave had dissipated on the street corner. I left for school feeling very sad, wishing—not for the last time—that my original idea were true. That all you had to do was live with a man, touch one another from time to time, on the hand or on the head, and sleep in the same bed, and the rest was entirely out of your control.

David and I took a second European holiday in 1980, and for the first time since my marriage, the morning we slipped into Oslo

Fjord on a steamer from Copenhagen, I neglected to use my diaphragm. We returned home resolved not to begin anything but to stop using birth control. Some of our friends to whom we confided our first step found this irresponsible. We claimed, and still do, that rather than backing in we had merely figured out how to wade into our next decision.

In January 1981, a yeast infection sent me to a gynecologist who yawned through the visit until he began taking a history. Intrigued by my menstrual irregularities, he asked if I had considered having children. Was he reading my mind? He informed me that I was a perfect candidate for a new drug that could virtually guarantee conception and he'd happily prescribe it as soon as I said the word. "We can have you pregnant before the year is out," he promised, sounding just like a fast-talking mechanic of a car in for servicing.

I said I wasn't quite ready yet. "Whenever," he replied, no longer interested. He gave me a new temperature chart; I still had my old basal thermometer. Greatly relieved about my prospects, I hurried home.

My husband grew upset at the first mention of the drug. "We're not up to that yet," he said.

"At least we know we have possibilities," I said. Then I paused. "He also said you could come in for a sperm count. Just to get that finished with."

"No way," he said. And then he wasn't in the mood for further conversation.

An out-of-town friend spent the day visiting the neighborhood in which he had grown up, the schools he attended, and the apartment house he and his mother lived in immediately after his parents' bitter divorce. Over dinner at our house he asked, "How can you even think of it?" He meant having children. "Kids are so vulnerable; they're subject to every kind of hurt. What makes you think you can handle all that responsibility? Are you sure?"

I wasn't at all sure I was ready, I patiently explained; I could only hope so. He didn't think that was enough, so I set out to convince him. "You're a different person than your parents were," I said. "You've learned from their mistakes."

"Child abusers were abused children," he told me, a journalist sure of his sources. "We repeat mistakes; we don't correct them."

At age twelve I began a diary for the express purpose of ensuring that I didn't commit the same outrages against my own children that my parents were busily committing against me. All their mistakes are well chronicled: the dress they found inappropriate, the English teacher they thought was trying to seduce me by sending me philosophy books, the time my mother read my diary. Years of traumas and family friction are recorded with such venom that today I can scarcely bear to read my harsh condemnations. Yet the family survived. And wasn't my eagerness to perpetuate the cycle evidence that my parents, despite all our battle scars, had done more right than wrong?

But my friend's parents had engraved in him a pain so acute that they made him unable to contend with his own troubles, stifled his procreative urges, frightened him from ever fathering someone else's hurt. "You'll do better than your parents," I said all the more urgently. "You have to. You have to believe in yourself that much."

"I don't," he said. "I just don't."

I did. Trying to untangle the knot of motivation which left me utterly convinced that I would succeed as a parent was this fact: I loved myself, I believed in myself, I knew I could do better than my parents. And it seemed only fair to take a stab, having overseen my own growing up with such intensity—keeping those diaries, documenting my development—to be the shaper instead of the clay. It was as if I had taken my mother's words, "You should only go through with your own daughter what you're doing to me," quite literally.

Otherwise, whenever I tried to articulate why I wanted children, I bumped my head on clichés. I wanted to create with my husband someone to whom we could be as important as our parents were to us. I wanted intimacy on a still-larger scale, a familial scale, the kind of pervasive, inviolate intimacy and density of emotions that is a family. I imagined our child as the maker of new relationships—turning my parents into grandparents, my sister into an aunt. Our child would be the best we had to offer in the way of creativity, artistry, sensitivity, individuality, bravery.

This sounds very noble. But mostly I wanted a child because my strongest desire was to experience myself as a mother. In no other way could I channel the energy I felt gathering in my body. It wouldn't be exorcised by perfecting my backhand, running a seven-minute mile, writing a novel, or traveling to remote mountain ranges. The love I knew was waiting for my baby couldn't be diverted to my husband, sister, friends, or parents. Having a child was a more final, more complete way of knowing myself, and the need for this kind of knowledge made me thirsty. In high school, I cried when I learned that a close friend had had sex with her boyfriend. Such a huge gulf separated us from then on; what she knew about what went on between men and women made what I knew seem trivial and shamefully naive. I coveted her knowledge, as I now coveted children, aware that loving a child is perhaps the closest we come to sanctioning self-love.

But it wasn't the right time. When I sounded sure, my husband paused, and when he waxed enthusiastic, I reined him in. Then an old high school friend living in Detroit called from the hospital the day after she gave birth. I cried to hear her, a reaction that surprised both her and me. David found my tears frightening.

A week later, when I proposed to him that I begin taking the magic drug in September, he told me to slow down. I revealed my master plan: conceive in October, deliver in May, resume teaching in September . . .

"You're pushing things," he said firmly. "No pills for at least another year. Let's just see what happens."

He sounded unshakable. With spring vacation approaching, I needed a project to burn off my disappointment and decided to restore the apartment—to strip away the layers of paint from the doors and window sashes to reveal the dark grained wood. By Monday morning I'd purchased the malodorous chemicals and rubber gloves, and was planning to begin with the painted-over French doors. But first we made love. And I conceived.

2

The First Trimester

Cross Currents

WHEN I FOUND OUT that I was pregnant, I wasn't standing dreamy-eyed by the window, calling my husband to say, "Darling, I have the most wonderful news." He was right beside me, and his expression of shock, incredulity, and wonder is forever etched on my mind. We had hardly spoken when the phone rang —a close friend. "It's positive, right?" she asked. "That's terrific. You must be so excited."

I honestly couldn't say *what* we were feeling: astonishment, certainly, never having expected to conceive with such ease. And muted excitement, as if we had just received a long awaited, fragile, intricately wrapped gift which would take us months to unpack. Yet in part I felt—while not unenthusiastic—somewhat at bay. "What now?" I asked my husband, but he only echoed my question back to me. Fortunately the phone rang again and an embarrassed nurse said, "I forgot to ask. Are you keeping the baby?"

"Yes, of course," I said, the significance of the moment registering for the first time. "But now what happens?" Laughing, she told me to come in for an examination.

It was midday; I had been in the middle of fixing lunch, but now the day's shape was altered. We decided to take a walk but didn't leave the house for nearly an hour and then never reached our intended destination, the park, where we had discussed so many of our future plans. Instead we walked on Broadway. The afternoon was hazy and warm, the street crowded with people on missions—buying fruit, cashing checks. We walked aimlessly, past luncheonettes and drugstores, holding hands, then not, wondering what came next.

Our only decision that afternoon—to refrain from sharing the news until a more reliable diagnosis could be made—was reversed by the time the phone rates went down that night. "My pregnancy test came out positive," I said to family and closest friends, carefully sidestepping any mention of a baby, cautiously balancing our fragile fears and happiness. No one seemed to notice. Most people, too fearful to be other than joyful, sounded thrilled, happier than I did. I felt like begging them to calm down, reminding them that the first trimester is a very risky time, that anything could happen. But to those who out of fear needed to sound reserved I wanted to cry, "Don't you tell me about caution, not yet. I know all the risks, but for now, can't you simply rejoice with us?"

The evening ended in tears. For me, the phone calls were an irreparable, regrettable mistake. I did not feel anyone had the right to be happier or more cautious than I was. "What did you expect?" my husband asked. I wasn't sure; I only knew I hadn't gotten it. Our privacy was shattered, our news made public, and no one had reacted correctly. I knew I was being difficult, expecting the impossible, disappointed beyond fairness.

Pregnancy is like adolescence—a circumscribed, transitional period riddled with ambivalence, a set-apart, self-conscious time which draws attention to itself, occasioning great shows of opinion and theory, but which finally must be simply endured. My reaction to the phone calls was reminiscent of my teenage years; the only major difference was that now I was alone.

Spoiled by my chronological adolescence during the 1960s, which I shared with millions, I was nonplussed and afraid to find myself crawling into the tunnel of pregnancy without cohorts from whom I could take my cues. Even my husband, disqualified by reasons of biology, wasn't allowed in the dark, uncertain space with me, but walked alongside me in the sunny, predictable world. And because so few of my friends were having children or were even close to making that decision, I couldn't sustain the illusion which comforted me as a teenager that we were all in this together. I was at once a role model, test case, pioneer, and oddity, a source of both awe and alienation. "You won't stop working?" my friends asked me, in a poignant tone combining both hope and warning. "You won't stop running?" "You won't stop being fun?" they asked time and time again, questions always phrased in the negative, eager for my assurance that no, nothing would change. You won't let happen to you what we most fear will happen to us, will you?

In counterpoint to their concerns came a barrage of well-intentioned but unsolicited advice, anecdotes, old wives' tales, tips and pointers from those for whom pregnancy was nothing special, something I could easily learn about by following their example. My women relatives and older women friends automatically assumed that I would do as they had done. All rites of passage have such attendants and engender expectations. I well remembered how my decision to get married had set in motion such a flurry of activity that my husband and I were lost in the ensuing roller coaster, our own desires subsumed and deflected.

But our wedding, however festive, paled beside the biggest shared drama of our lives which would unfold over the next nine months. To rely on the impressions and experiences of others would be to cheat ourselves. We wanted to discard the script of conventional responses and discover how we were feeling together and independently; we had to assimilate the news in a strictly personal way, to acknowledge and accept all our feelings and label them with our own names.

This would entail walking the cutting edge, rejecting neither the old nor the new ways completely, embracing neither whole-heartedly. As much as I horrified my elders by insisting on exercise, work, and as normal a life as possible, I betrayed my contemporaries by refusing to think of my pregnancy as a mere interruption.

I felt both exhilarated and fearful, both in and hopelessly out of step with the stereotype of the newly pregnant woman, willing to fight and succumb, eager to model a new kind of woman yet happy to take my place in the generational line-up, behind my mother and her mother.

Nothing I read and no one I consulted focused on ambivalence to the extent and degree that I was experiencing it. Those who alluded to it at all did so fleetingly, reluctantly, as if they wished they didn't have to. I was familiar enough with this tack, having long practiced the art of lying, distorting, evading. Impressions and expectations had always been more important to me than emotional honesty. But the reality of being pregnant seemed so singular, so enormous, that I felt powerless to lie, almost compelled beyond my will to be truthful.

That most women on the verge of bearing children felt as I did seemed without question. But our concerns remained voiceless in oral and written literature because unambivalent accounts are easier to write—and to live.

As long as I was cast as a pioneer, I began taking that role seriously and resorted to the strategy I had used to keep my balance during an adolescence I had taken equally seriously: I began keeping a diary. If no brutally honest account existed, I'd write my own.

The first entry is dated May 25, a full two weeks after the pregnancy test. Each morning I woke up from my own private summer, the fetus a tiny power source elevating my body temperature, making me sweat and steam. At my desk sandwiched between two windows, I watched workers remove masonry from a building across the alley and looked not ahead but back: no wonder I had been so highly strung about the dinner party I had thrown a month ago;

no wonder my running had been so tough; no wonder I had picked a fight with David the night of the pregnancy test. But even as the pieces of the past fell into place, the future became scrambled. I was scheduled to teach a course this summer, to run a mini-marathon in two weeks, to rent a cabin on Cape Cod, to spend weekends and all of August in the Berkshires—certainly nothing spectacular, not the way we would have chosen to spend our last summer together. This was supposed to be a summer devoted to work; next summer was time for the before–baby extravaganza vacation . . .

"There's still time," David said, the only evening we broached the subject out loud, together. We could shirk responsibilities, spend our savings instead of augment them, and simply take off. Independently, we both entertained such reckless, romantic notions and decided that it would be only an empty gesture. What was growing inside me had already changed us—this was to be a summer of beginnings, not endings. We were no longer alone. To quiet the part of me that still felt cheated, I borrowed one moment from last summer's month-long trip to Scandinavia.

We were on a late afternoon boat ride into the Stockholm archipelago with our hosts—Fred, an American whom I had known in college, and his wife, Elisabeth, a Swede. Most people on the boat weren't tourists but commuters who worked in the city and summered on the islands. Island is actually an exaggeration; they were tiny mushrooms of land capped by traditional Swedish country homes—red boxes with white trim, flagpoles, and neat gardens, often one per island. Our conversation wasn't memorable until we approached the farthest port on our route. As the afternoon lengthened, Elisabeth began describing the miscarriage she had suffered earlier that spring, and Fred remarked how ironic it was that if that pregnancy had come to term, as they had wished, none of us would be here now. "We plan to travel with Little Baby Charles," David said—our code word for our hypothetical child, still only a dream, a joke, a lifetime away.

"Are you trying to tell us something?" Fred asked.

"Not at all," I assured him. "Not yet."

"Well," he went on, "it's reasonable to assume that the next time we see each other we'll all have children along."

The boat was completing its circle to head home and a bevy of swans settled in the arc of our wake—a chilling moment, the exact point at which the summer and our lives cracked. I felt the presence of children and shuddered, not only because of the wind, not only because we were in exotic waters, Finland and the Soviet Union as close as they had ever been, but because of the shadow his prophecy had cast.

We ate that night in the ship's dining room, a splurge that David and I rarely indulge in on vacation. We, who normally sleep on deck and eat out of bags and boxes while on line for tickets for something else, who rough it and flaunt our thriftiness, sat down to linen tablecloths and napkins and elegantly prepared food served on bone china. The sun was setting, from the porthole Fred spotted a Russian trawler; we relaxed in the glow of wine, sun, wind, good fellowship, and drank a farewell toast to it all.

Our first social event of the season was the annual party for my husband's graduate school program. David solicitously deposited me at an outdoor table, far from the nauseating mounds of food, and promised he'd tell only his closest friends. I sipped club soda and watched the drizzly evening darken over the low rooftops surrounding Washington Square Park. Slowly, friends began dropping by, as if paying court, to offer congratulations. Then others began arriving, people I didn't know well, including one woman in her eighth month who was bursting with twins. She chatted to me while rubbing her stomach as if to erode it. I caught glimpses of David, tie loosened, shaking hands, hugging and being hugged, his face beaming, unable to keep the news to himself.

Outside, I felt like an impostor waiting to be found out, half-expecting someone I didn't know to challenge me: You don't look pregnant. Did I feel different only because I expected to?

Prospective parents are instant celebrities, and I had little time to think. Everyone who stopped by had something to say on the subject of childbirth—even those without children spoke authoritatively, while single men sounded reverential, as if I had done something terribly original. Women with children long out of diapers were generous with advice, and quick to assure me that their doctor was the best in the city, the hospital at which they delivered equipped with the best nursing staff in the state. But then in the middle of these otherwise informative conversations each woman's face grew wistful: "My first pregnancy was the best time of my life." The chairman of the department echoed this sentiment when he stopped by, adding that he and his wife were among the first to choose natural childbirth when it was all new, exciting, vaguely subversive. "It was a great time," he said. "Everyone we knew was pregnant; every woman in our building, everyone in the park."

This was, I suppose, intended to cheer me. Hadn't he noticed, as I had, that in a room full of eminent candidates for motherhood most were eating heartily, planning internships, dissertation studies, field trips? Wasn't it obvious that aside from me and the expectant mother of twins, there was only one other set of young parents in the room—the only people I wanted to talk to, my unformulated questions multiplying in my mind—and they were so busy entertaining their one-year-old daughter that they couldn't stop by my table to say anything at all?

Our next party was a smaller, more intimate one, dinner at my mother's with my aunt and grandmother. It was the first time I had seen them since our announcement. I felt immediately besieged by matriarchal wisdom: Don't let the doctor examine you, it's too early; stop running; stop working; rest; cancel all travel plans; don't take even an aspirin; don't expect life to ever be the same; no one slides off the delivery table with skinny thighs.

I knew that we were being welcomed into an old club, shown the secret handshake, prepared for the final initiation. David and I kicked each other under the table as my aunt rhapsodized about breast feeding: "It's the closest relationship you ever have with anyone. It's like nothing else." My mother, who hadn't breast-fed either of her daughters, was stony-faced.

After dinner, when everyone but my parents had adjourned to the living room, my mother put on her listen-up tone and said, "I just have one thing to tell you." She'd been rehearsing this a long time. "The baby is yours. No matter what happens . . ."

"Stop it," I shouted. "I don't know what you're trying to say but I don't want to hear it. The baby is mine and David's. It takes two."

My father, clearing the dishes, tried to intervene: "All your mother means . . ." but I wouldn't listen, especially to him. Didn't he realize he was once the outsider himself, the man against whom my mother's mother must have cautioned her?

My anger, which flustered us all, was far from spent. I knew I was being unfair taking my mother's words literally when she hadn't meant them as such. Surely she had intended no personal affront to David, but was merely saying the words she thought mothers ought to say, what she had been told at her mother's kitchen table. But if she had never examined what motivated such an admonition, I would. Her advice stemmed from an older, divisive notion of sexual roles, from a deep past when pregnancy and childbirth were the only realms women had to themselves, which they had to protect with a fierce jealousy. This was a legacy from which I recoiled. My baby would not be the cornerstone upon which my self-esteem would rest. David would be my partner in childrearing, not a threatening presence.

"I don't know what I was trying to say," she said, apologizing for hurting me, though she wasn't sure exactly how. "That's okay," I said, hoping she wouldn't figure it out for either of our sakes.

Later, I realized that as much as I felt ambushed by my relatives' brand of advice, it was not only predictable but mostly ritual, offered in an impersonal, almost nonpersonal way. They were in part simply discharging a duty, perhaps unwittingly avenging their own having to sit through similar sessions with their mothers. Much less expected was the advice offered by younger friends. "You'll do Lamaze, of course," they said. "You'll keep your job. . . . We took our baby to Europe when he was three. . . . We took our daughter camping when she was four. . . . It's easy to integrate a baby into your life."

My sister Annie called. She was single, childless, but eager to help me compose a list of questions to ask all the obstetricians I planned on interviewing: What percentage of the babies you deliver are Cesarean births? At what point do you induce labor? Do you deliver the baby onto the mother's belly? Does the hospital in which you have privileges use sugar water in the nursery? I paused between each item, but wrote not a word. These were all reasonable requests. At an earlier time I would have done the same for her, for any of my friends, but now all I could think was, "If you only knew how not up to this I am. If you only knew how sleepy I feel."

I wanted a doctor to come to me, or else I wanted everyone I asked to have used the same wonderful doctor so that I could make only one call. I didn't want to conduct interviews, to make decisions; I had used up all my assertiveness battling my grandmother's old wives' tales, and hadn't any left to combat my feminist sisters: especially since I agreed with them as wholeheadedly, if not wholeheartedly, as I would have if I were my old self. But I wasn't; I was changing and I needed someone to understand, accept, and allow me my overwhelming passivity. All advice, politically correct or not, took on the cold hue of a battle cry. Everyone seemed to be asking if I was for or against issue after issue. Never had I realized how many issues were involved.

"We'll be pregnant for nine long months," I told my sister, asking if she couldn't relent, take a moment to read me.

"Wait a second," she said. "*You're* the only one that's pregnant."

I began to feel as if I were flunking Feminism 101.

None of the pleasures turned up where I expected them. I existed in a state of nearly continual unease, anticipating what didn't come, almost missing the sweetness which always arrived when and where I wasn't looking. My friend from the Midwest, whose daughter's birth inspired my conceiving, sent me a package containing a tiny white outfit. Stitched in yellow across the bib was "Little Me." "She's already outgrown this," my friend wrote, "(Can you believe it?) and I thought you'd like to hold onto it." I kept it out all day but when David came home he glanced at it and barked, "Put it away." I reminded him that we had decided not to be superstitious, but he insisted. I buried it deep in my underwear drawer.

Accompanying the package was a note. "Babies are cute," my friend had written, next to a circled number one. Item number two read, "Babies are time-consuming. I can barely take time to brush my teeth without her screaming for my attention. But I'm sure after just a few weeks your baby will be content to stay in his crib and relax with a good book." I laughed, and reread her note to see what she had placed between the lines, what encoded message she had sent me. But there was nothing else. Babies are cute but demanding.

On the day that I was to have run the ten-kilometer race in Central Park, David and I went to the thirtieth-birthday picnic of a man with whom he had grown up. The friend had a three-year-old daughter and within a month would have another. It was perfect softball weather, and the men galloped off to a game. At any other time in my life I would have joined them. Instead, I lingered at the picnic site with the women and babies, none of whom I knew well. Children of all ages were crawling everywhere, demanding, crying, getting dirty, while mothers compared notes about diapers, rashes, hemorrhoids, and operations.

The hostess found me trying to escape the nauseating smell of barbecued hamburgers. "You're not eating," she said. I should have told her that I too was pregnant, but couldn't. She had her daughter's lunch smeared on her blouse. I'd never join these ranks. Not one of the babies was cute and all the mothers looked like caricatures. Even after I found out that the prime offender was a practicing attorney, I couldn't shake the image of her as someone not only uninteresting but repellent. I felt like crying, said nothing to the woman who sought me out, wanted what had been done undone, coveted the body of a fourteen-year-old, craved no hips, no breasts, and wished that I were anywhere else, on the softball field, even striking out.

I worried constantly about fetal demise, that at any second whatever microscopic mechanism was so bravely and against all odds pumping away might be snuffed out. I worried too about chromosomal damage that could have already been cast, evading any subsequent correction. I had been in smoke-filled bars, and had had a cigarette the week after I conceived; I had sipped brandy at a party the day after I conceived; I had used dangerous chemicals in the apartment the day of conception. I didn't take vitamins and had only recently sworn off my three-cup-a-day coffee habit. From my Midwest friend had come a book with a cheery title, something like *Let's Eat Right During Pregnancy*—as if eating at all during pregnancy weren't problematic enough. The book advocated cleansing the body of all poisonous substances for a year or two before trying to conceive.

"You have less to worry about than anyone else I know," a friend told me during the dinner to which she was treating me by way of celebration. Generously, she ordered a bottle of white wine. I said I wasn't drinking.

"Come on," she insisted, "just a toast." I thought of the cesspool of my blood. When I took a sip I wished I could discreetly spit it out, as I had done with vegetables as a child.

At the next table sat a young couple with a two-year-old daughter, valiantly trying to dine normally as the girl grabbed food, whined, squirmed, and cried. "Is that what you want?" my friend asked. "In two years that will be you. Are you sure?"

"Sure," I thought to myself. Who could ever be sure? I was sure I *thought* that that was what I wanted. Was that enough?

"Coffee?" the waiter asked. My friend nodded but I refused.

"Oh come on," my friend said. "You can carry this purity business too far. Think of teenage mothers. All they eat is potato chips and cola."

"I know," I replied. My aunt had told me she couldn't keep anything down during all three of her pregnancies, and her children were doing fine. But that didn't finally matter at all. I was trying to calculate odds. If there was, please, dear God, no defect already built in and cruelly flowering at this very moment, the least I could do was swallow the appropriate substances.

"Just water for me," I said.

What were the odds that my baby would be healthy? How would I—could I—in fact cope with anything less than a perfect form? Each healthy, whole face on a bus seemed to increase the odds that my baby might not be; every other pregnant woman became a kind of threat. It must happen to someone, I thought, it could be me.

This incessant, imprecise recitation of the odds against the chance that something could go wrong, could already be wrong, was like a smell that remained inside my nose.

"You must be so excited," people squealed, I suppose because we are led to believe that is what we should say, but I kept wishing they wouldn't treat me like a character in a situation comedy who does nothing but knit until the baby shower. "I'm perpetually worried," I'd say.

"About what?" Were they playing dumb? Eventually I was able to force myself to say the words aloud: birth defects. Fetal demise. I assumed that if I brought it up, the least people could do was listen. I didn't expect comfort, certainly not guarantees; just simple acknowledgment. Yes, that is a reality, a real fear. Instead, people shuddered, said, "Don't worry," as if it were possible not to, and turned away looking shocked, as if I had belched loudly or sounded like a garden-variety party pooper.

"But you look great," they said, ignoring my comment that I had never felt worse. "Are you nauseated? Do you throw up?"

I hadn't. I felt encouraged to divulge my physical discomforts in great detail. People seemed interested in these facts. I couldn't stand chicken or eggs. The least trace of fattiness made me gag. I retched midway through just about every meal.

"It must be awful," they said sympathetically.

What was awful was thinking about the time bomb ticking inside me, something new developing, perhaps misfiring, every second. The fetus already had brain waves, hair. It was a luxury to talk about physical discomforts. Cravings? Sure, I had them. I wanted ice cream constantly. Hold the pickles.

We dwell on physical symptoms because no one wants to hear the ticking. No one wants to think about the tiny invader growing second by second in my belly, the creature slated to cause greater happiness and greater despair than anything else in my life until now.

"Do you have stretch marks?" a cousin asked. "I have a great cream which gets rid of them absolutely."

One morning, David woke up and waved at my stomach, introducing himself to the bulge. When a friend called and said, "I'd like to speak to the fetus of the family," David replied, "Sorry, he can't come to the phone right now. He's cleaning his womb."

Nights I lay awake on my back, wishing someone could plot for me the position of the baby on a set of axes. It was placed so terribly internally, beyond the probing fingers of an examiner, in a noiseless, dark, buried chamber which had always been there, but in which, until now, I had never lived.

My running partner called. "Beth and I had a talk about you," she said. "I think she's more upset because she doesn't want to have kids." When Beth called, she said my running partner was more upset because she knows she wants kids. What everyone was thinking was that with this new person about to enter my life, I might not have time for my friends. "Will you be fun any more?" "I feel as if I have to treasure every letter from you because soon you won't be able to write." "Will there be any room left for us?"

Reassurances worked, but in fact I was inhabiting the most unneedy phase of my life. Neither asleep nor awake, my eyes were either open or closed, but my trancelike state remained the same. I could rouse myself to do errands, but they exhausted me in ways that were not purely physical. I spent weeks of sultry afternoons in the house feeling ambitionless. For the first time in my life I felt no need to do the things I had always felt a pronounced need to do, no need to cultivate what I had always tended out of a mixture of discipline, obsession, and drive. What I felt now resembled contentment.

Forgetting friends, conversation, work, diversion, I would stretch out on the sofa. I began reading books about the Holocaust, a subject I had fastidiously eschewed before, and I listened to Mozart and Bach. But when the side of the record was finished or a page needed turning, I could easily let the record stop, the book fall, watch the long rays of light pour in through the dusty windows, the shadows collect in the corners. David would come home to find me dozing. He brought the newspaper which I ignored, cooked dinner I couldn't look at, and ate with gusto while I wished that nutrition—the required grams of protein—could be injected into my body in a manner bypassing my taste buds, digestive tract, and stomach. He reminded me of chores that needed tending, including finding an obstetrician. I waited for the fin of whatever was swimming around in the tropical, ever-expanding pool I provided to tickle my stomach.

No one knew the extent to which thoughts of the baby consumed me, not even David. Its image, when visible, was primitive, and floated around the inside of my eyes. I conscientiously avoided talking about my preoccupation too much, thinking that if encouraged I could go on for hours. But when a friend asked why I *didn't* talk about it more, I realized I didn't want to. It was as tranquil a time as I had ever known, my emotions fed from an utterly secret and new source.

Equally secret were the books I read about the Holocaust, one after the other, which were absorbed but never discussed. As sunny as that season was, in one room of my mind the shades were always down and someone was chanting an incessant prayer for the dead, parents and children.

By my tenth week, I had assembled a list of about ten doctors, all promised to be the best in the city. I had to choose one. Realizing,

after too many weeks had elapsed, that one wasn't about to magi-
cally appear, I selected three by a process I couldn't articulate and
made appointments for consultations. One receptionist, with a
heavy eastern European accent, had the most pleasant telephone
manner I'd ever encountered. She was able to arrange an appoint-
ment for the following day—very convenient, I told my husband.
But did that mean that the practice was small, perhaps of poor
repute?

The basement-level waiting room of Dr. Christina Peters was
dominated by four huge canvases of muted colors blending into
gray. The receptionist urged us to ignore the magisterial cat dozing
in the center of the rug. The rooms were cool and narrow; I felt
as if I were on a ship.

The doctor's own office was dark and lined with books. On
her desk were scattered countless pictures of babies in individual,
miniature frames. Dr. Peters had a Swedish accent, blunt-cut blond
hair, and the manner of a kindly admiral. I showed her my temperature chart. She studied it, took a brief medical history, explained her
procedures—if I decided to use her, she would soon send me for
a sonogram—and told us to think clearly. This was an important
decision.

I left with many questions. Why was no one else in the waiting
room? Why would I have to go for a sonogram? Perhaps she was
too interventionist? I hadn't asked her any of the questions my
sister had suggested. Although she came highly recommended, I
had appointments the following week with two other doctors
whose practices were huge, whose receptionists were cold, whose
offices were on the other side of town. David and I debated the
entire ride home, but at five minutes to five I called Dr. Peters's
office to say that I was coming aboard.

At my first regular office visit, Dr. Peters informed me that she
wanted a sonogram quickly. Two days later I lay undressed and
shivering on the cold metal table of the radiologist who was about
to perform the ultrasound. I had drunk over a quart of water in the

past hour so that my full bladder would prop up my uterus to make it more photogenic. I dreamed of going to the bathroom.

A cold gel was applied to my abdomen and I was scanned with a wand which transmitted squiggly white lines, like interference on a TV screen, to a machine on my right where my husband stood. "That," said the radiologist, "is the primitive spinal cord, and that is the head," indicating nothing more than a dense field of snow on the screen. He told us that fetal age was about ten weeks, and swore, in response to all our questions, that he couldn't tell us anything else about how normal fetal development was. "You're calmer than he is," the doctor told me, regarding my husband, as if this surprised him.

When I was dressed and my bladder empty, we met in the doctor's office where he had displayed several pictures of the fetus on a lighted wall. "Congratulations," he said, shaking our hands. "I hope you have a boy. They're easier to raise."

A week later, at the obstetrician's, we were told that the sonogram exactly confirmed Dr. Peters's own calculations of due date, which she computed anew each visit on a rotating disc. The fetus was precisely eleven weeks old. Did I have any questions?

Could I run? She thought not. Even if it did no harm, the jostling couldn't do any good. "Swim," she said.

I hated swimming. I didn't know what to do. Friends regaled me with stories of women they knew who knew women whose friends trained for marathons while pregnant, who ran marathons in their eighth month, who played three sets of tennis before jogging to the hospital to deliver. What they were trying to suggest, I think, was that if running was not universally contraindicated, I should keep at it. Rustling up no small amount of courage, I replied that it was hard enough choosing a doctor; I wasn't about to go against her advice. Instead, I bought goggles and found a red leotard and began swimming at an indoor pool each noon.

Since I had never learned properly, my strokes were inefficient and my distance meager. But I built up, increasing the number of laps and time in the water, learned to navigate the busy lanes, and diverted myself by watching to see whose bathing suit was slipping off.

I must have been a good show in my own right—my belly swelling the leotard to near bursting. I felt like a whale, or a human iceberg, with more bulk below than above the water. After completing my required number of laps, I'd take one more floating on my back at a relaxed pace, in the slow lane, and it was here, one afternoon, with the sound of muted conversation seeping in and out of my ears as the water level rose and fell, that I realized this was the one time of day during which my baby and I were engaged in the same activity.

"You're looking more womanly," my mother-in-law reported. "You look voluptuous," said a friend. "Like an Italian movie star," added my husband. Clothes still fit but I had to buy new bras. I wished I were enormous so I could believe, all the time, in the reality of the baby. We purchased a book of photographs *in utero* and held its pages to my belly each week. When the book promised that now the fetus was as long as a phone receiver, we solemnly placed one at my navel, and imagined the rest. The proof the sonogram had offered was waning: too visual, too static. Life is movement and we needed a kick.

"Don't you wish you could be pregnant?" I asked David one sweltering night when neither of us could sleep. "Don't you wish you could experience the drama of a human life developing inside you?" He said he didn't. No wonder. He knew as well as I did the changes the pregnancy had brought, could accurately describe the toll it exacted on me and our relationship and catalogue the sacrifices: constant, if minimal seasickness; no iced coffee, cold beers, or aspirin for headaches; no late nights; too much sleep, food, lethargy, and self-absorption. My figure was become liquescent, spreading perhaps past the point of no return.

"You never looked better," barked a great-uncle at a family party, using the same tone of voice with which he had once instructed his daughter to clean her room. "You have an inner glow." Clearly he was lying; what was it about my condition that scared him into uttering nonsense? Maybe years ago, when women were becoming pregnant in droves, sharing morning sickness, diaper pins, and comfort, pregnancy was the best time of their lives. Perhaps this was their first excuse to pay attention to their bodies, to take care of themselves. All I felt was restricted and exhausted by relentless attention to bodily functions—ingestion, digestion, excretion—all accelerated, all working for two.

"I feel invaded," I complained to my husband. "I worry that I can't think of one thing that isn't connected to this pregnancy. I complain too much." Assuring me that I didn't, David turned over and went to sleep. Even though he had begun lingering near Little League games, staring at children hoisted on their fathers' shoulders, eavesdropping on children's conversations on buses, and studying the parents' books we received, I worried that his reluctance to fantasize about becoming pregnant himself was my fault. If I weren't so negative, he'd be freer to see beyond the complaints. For buried amid the discomforts and disgust was an untrammeled delight, the nature of which I couldn't fashion into words, but which was wholly enviable. I could sense it best when I didn't try to. Maybe the negative feelings were easier to dwell on because to admit this excitement was to expose new depths of potential disappointment and hurt. These weeks constituted the most extreme terrain I had ever inhabited, all caused by a twelve-week-old fetus whose very existence was so fragile and elusive that we depended on interpreters and electronic equipment to bring it to us.

"The first trimester is the hardest time," everyone assured us. "Just survive the first three months and you'll be fine." As much as I wanted to believe the network of women who brought me this news, I couldn't. They were wrong about everything else, and had exhausted their credibility.

With one gloved hand on my abdomen, the other inside, my doctor said not to me but to the nurse, "A well-established pregnancy. Very well established." She patted me on the stomach as she grasped a wand which would detect the heartbeat, if everything was right—please, please. First she applied a gel, then clicked on a hand-held amplifier. We heard nothing but placental sounds of a deep, inner sea. After a heart-stopping interval, I heard it, like a motor, an engine, fast and loud. "That's it," the doctor said. "Please get my husband," I asked the nurse, and a moment later he came rushing in, his watch set to take the baby's pulse.

"It's fast," he said. "Over one hundred sixty beats a minute," the doctor said, clicking off her machine. "Healthy, very healthy."

In her office she used words like excellent, perfect, fine— superlatives we drank into our skin. She told me to keep doing whatever I was doing, and come back in a month. My biweekly visits were over.

My husband had to leave for work, looking more excited than I had seen him look in weeks, and I walked home alone through the park—a sunny, nearly flawless day—on the gravel path along the reservoir, with the words "well established" running through my head like a mantra. A line of gulls had settled on the jetty, which looked like the minute hand of a giant clock. One day, I thought, I'll retrace these steps with my child and say, "This is where I first believed in you." I cried, too, for the first time, conjuring the presence next to me, a tiny hand in mine, a head at my waist, my hem at my baby's shoulders. "Thank you, thank you," I cried silently to my doctor, interpreter of sounds and vials of blood, possessor of magic wands who interprets my body to me. I would live in her office if I could and use her machines every day. How would I manage for an entire month on my own?

When even my baggiest jeans and wrap-around skirts made me hold my breath, we went to a maternity boutique. I fully expected to be greeted with the same snickers I had heard sixteen years ago, purchasing my first bra. But to the saleswoman I was Madam Dear; she directed me to jeans with a spandex panel that fit so comfortably I sighed as audibly as my grandmother does removing her girdle. I bought one pair. On the bus ride home, the bag on my lap attracted the eye of a young man in a three-piece suit who came right over and said, "You're pregnant! I have a three-month-old son at home and I can't tell you how much I miss him and I've only been away since last night." He told us details of his wife's C-section, the baby's Apgar score (9), and how he hadn't realized how badly he wanted a boy until the doctor told him he had a son, and then he made the doctor tell him again and again. When he got off the bus, everyone was looking at us and smiling.

That night, when David and I went out for dessert, I told him I'd never heard of an Apgar score before; now I had something new to worry about. "Just the first of many tests," he said. I was wearing my new pants, and in them I looked pregnant. Even hanging in my closet, they instantly acquired a magical significance: They belonged to a pregnant woman.

Walking past the hospital in which I would deliver, I saw a nurse settle a new mother and newborn into the front seat of a car while the father, nervously fidgeting on the sidelines, concentrated as if the baby's existence depended on his gaze. I stopped and said aloud, "Some day that will be me." But the words had trouble penetrating.

I met a friend for lunch. After admiring my belly and asking me when I was due, she said, "And I'm due the month after." It took several moments for her news to sink in. I hugged and congratulated her, careful to note in her face the same apprehensions, doubts, fears, dismay, and helplessness I had lived with for so many weeks but which were suddenly—or not so suddenly—gone. Her troubled face was a mirror in which I saw not how I looked now but where I'd been. My first trimester ended in that gaze.

"The first three months are the hardest," I assured her, not knowing what was ahead, but knowing I no longer felt as bad as she looked. How I hated the sound of my voice giving at the first opportunity the advice I had so hated receiving. I needed to assure her that even though I sounded like everyone else with worthless advice, she shouldn't be fooled: This was the honest truth.

INDEPENDENCE DAY. David and I spent the Fourth of July weekend at his parents' country home in the Berkshires. The house, which my in-laws had purchased four years ago, soon after the death of their daughter, was a house free of ghosts, a house devoted entirely to the future. From the float on which I sunned like a beached whale, I studied it—a chalet painted brown and red like a cherry bonbon—and the narrow, sloping backyard. Four years ago we had selected sites where the future would unfold: here a sandbox, there swings, a basketball hoop near the flowers.

For the past three months, the future of which I was the curator had had my body in an uproar. Now, four days into my second trimester, I felt fine. I was larger, certainly, but intact, back to myself. Promised relief had come, just as everyone swore it would, exactly on schedule. Yet I found myself reluctant to accept the truce my body so generously offered. After all the work I'd done during my first trimester to stake out my own emotional territory, to define the experience of pregnancy in a personal way, the last words I expected to find myself writing in my journal were: "These days I feel so fulfilled, so contented."

"Oh God," I had moaned, shutting the book. "I'm turning into a cliché before my own eyes."

"Look," David offered, "if you feel better, you feel better. The books couldn't have been wrong about everything. Think of the law of percentages."

He had joined me on the float in the middle of the lake.

When we were first married, we referred to our long afternoons in bed as time spent on our raft; when the real world intervened, we made the raft portable—a state of mind. Here in Hinsdale, Massachusetts, we had found an actual raft on which to spend our last summer as a duo. It became our home. Aboard, although doubts about the pregnancy didn't evaporate, we experienced them more remotely, as if the interval between thought and reaction had lengthened. Communication from the outside world reached us, but only after slight, barely perceptible delays, much like the pauses that impede transcontinental phone calls. Time, which we couldn't lose track of in the spring, whose passing we discerned everywhere, became simply too tedious to measure. And the white noise which had until now accompanied us was entirely and inexplicably stilled. The only sounds we heard were disembodied voices from canoes nosing around the lake's perimeter. All that kept time was our running commentary to each other, as steady and comforting as a heartbeat.

I sat in our dark apartment, just home from teaching my summer school course which I hated. After only one session I was dreading the next. My left-over hippy clothes—skirts with elastic waistbands, floppy shirts—were in a puddle on the floor: I wouldn't wear maternity clothes to teach, didn't want anyone to know. Naked, I felt between identities. Waiting for David to return from his class, unwilling to light the lamp, I rubbed my stomach compulsively as if to apologize for subjecting it to too tight clothes, to fetid subway air, to being on my feet for so long writing notes about prepositions on the blackboard, for channeling energy to total strangers. I wished I didn't have to take my mind off . . . what? To sit home and think about the baby all day was to think about nothing. The only time the baby came to life was when it snuck through the side door of my mind as I was thinking about something else—prepositions—the way you can't see a star until you slightly avert your eyes.

David and I drove south to Washington, D.C., one weekend to visit Marian, the friend with whom I had been closest longest. We met in an eighth-grade English class and overcame not only our initial bad impressions of each other (she found me prissy, I found her condescending) but her marriage, divorce, my marriage, and many far-flung moves. What had always stayed constant throughout these outward changes was the quality of our contact, which left us both feeling replenished.

The last time I had visited Marian had been three years ago, before she moved to Utah. We stayed up way after our husbands went to sleep, smoking cigarettes, drinking wine—activities not in my repertoire since college when these attractions of the adult world made us dizzy.

"Well, you're certainly not going to drink or smoke this time," David said. I assured him I would be staying up late, with a defiant pout I hadn't used in years. It wasn't so much him I resented as his message: This visit was already too late to be the last of its kind. Despite all the changes Marian and I had withstood so far, nothing would prove as disruptive to our friendship as the protrusion in my stomach. The baby, more than any other single act or accident of adulthood, had already played havoc with how my friends and I related.

I conked out way before eleven, so Marian and I had our late Friday night talk on Saturday afternoon, strolling absently from cage to cage in the Washington Zoo.

She told me about the man she was seeing, the divorced father of two young boys. "He doesn't want any more children," she said sadly. "I think I do." I nodded sympathetically. "Actually, that's the least of our problems."

We paused at the home of the pandas, the couple with fertility and compatibility problems of their own. "Tell me everything," Marian said finally. "I want to hear it all."

So much of what we know of the important events in life—sex, death, birth—is vicarious. Marian and I had always pooled our knowledge, but frankly, I had always been the slower learner. She was the first one to make out, to marry, divorce, to experience the loss of loved ones. Unused to having the lowdown about anything, I was uncertain how to begin.

I knew her offer was genuine, that she realized I needed to talk and she needed to listen. She had been pursuing a career with admirable dedication for all the years that I had been settling into my relationship with David; she was a walking imploder of the myth of sexual stereotypes, just as I'd always thought I'd be. Instead, I was a prime example of one of the most insidious myths —the merrily pregnant. I suppose that in college we both imagined a future for ourselves in which we could both destroy and embody the roles we had grown up with. Now we were a bit puzzled to admit that we had had to choose, and couldn't remember ever making the choice. The anguished ambivalence of the months before would have been much easier to describe to one as modern as she was. But now that my fears had shifted into this new philosophical gear, how could I relay the contentment, the tickle, the thrill?

"You don't have to protect me," she said.

I simply felt so traditional. She envied my timetable, found her own to be dangerously late—she was a year older than I, with no husband, no immediate prospects, her biological clock always ticking away. Still, her interest and compassion outweighed her envy. No one else had been nearly so generous, asking for the whole story; and in truth, there was no one else I trusted it with.

Sparing no details, I told her of my newfound peacefulness,

my speculations on my suitability for motherhood. Reasonably confident that I could stimulate my baby, I worried about my ability to set limits.

"David will help you with that," she said. "That's what he does well." And I thought, Of course.

I said that I wasn't sure if I should teach in the spring after the birth or take a semester off.

"You'll need the time at home, I think." This also sounded right. When I said that I sometimes worried about being emotionally prepared, she said that she didn't know anyone with better emotional equipment to be a mother than I, though she said it much more beautifully than that.

Then, as if coaxing me backward, she got past my musings and gently allowed me to realize that I was still nurturing many doubts and fears about the baby's health, about accidents, abnormalities, which hadn't evaporated at all but were simply dormant for a while. She made me confront how much I feared for this child, how profound my love was, how tied up in my bones and blood the baby dwelt. "I worry that I won't ever feel the baby kick," I confessed, nearly in tears.

Marian took my arm and said a miraculous thing: that she had always known that my pregnancy was *beshert.* It was a word both our grandmothers had used to signify that which is right, ordained, blessed. And with that single word it was as if the wound she had so gently and lovingly opened a moment before was immediately staunched and healed. Perhaps the sound of the old word in her mouth reminded me that we too would be grandmothers, perhaps comfort came because I secretly believed as she did. But for whatever combination of reasons I put the fears about the baby's future in a dark room and closed the door. The whole enterprise was already blessed, everything as it should be. And this, from Marian, was my first baby gift.

We ended up getting lost in the bird section, walking past rows of cages, finally coming upon a cluster of kids, all cousins, I think, gathered around the ostrich family. "It's more fun to watch the kids than the animals," Marian said. Sure, they were endearing, remarking on the strangest things. But I, never before an animal lover, who always found children infinitely more interesting than birds, was entranced by the integrity of the animals themselves. While the kids hammed it up, the birds, in their mindless attention to what was purely biological mothering, comforted me. If they could do it, so could I.

Sunday brunch was a kind of reunion: Marian had invited Roger and Ruth, with whom we had gone to high school, and their ten-week-old son.

Ruth, still in maternity clothes, barely said "Hi" before kneeling on the floor of the living room to change the baby, using the flap of a diaper bag as a changing pad. As if it were a show-and-tell project, she talked throughout the procedure, demonstrating how to hold the baby's legs, use the wipes, apply ointment. Extracting a plastic bag like those found in supermarket produce departments, she explained, "I rip off hundreds of these." We all leaned closer to look. Not ten seconds later a soggy diaper taped upon itself into an inoffensive cube rested safe inside the knotted plastic bag, which she held aloft for a moment like a trophy before handing it to me to dump in the trash can.

During brunch we were treated to the unabridged story of her premature labor and delivery, a complex tale full of false starts and rapidly rising action, laced with the technology of childbirth— water breaking, induction. At her first pause I was prepared to say, "Look, don't do this on my account"—I was far more interested in the noodle pudding—but waiting for my opportunity I realized that this wasn't for my benefit at all. Eventually I tuned out, grateful that the narrative probably made it difficult for anyone else to keep track of how many bagels I was eating.

Roger held his son on his lap. The tiny Buddha-like creature made uncontrolled twitching movements, and seemed more unaware of his surroundings than the pandas I had seen yesterday in the zoo. That, I wondered, reaching for more pudding, that is the climax of this saga? That is what is in store for me?

Suddenly Ruth stopped in the middle of a sentence. "I feel the milk every two hours like clockwork," she said, scooping up her son and retreating to the den for what turned into an entire afternoon of nursing. I was appalled; I had no idea that it took so long. The last time I had been close enough to a nursing couple to hear the coos and sucks was when my aunt nursed my youngest cousin, now twenty, and that rests in my memory as a lickety-split operation.

Ruth opened her blouse, put her feet up, and began talking to me. I had followed her in, as if in thrall, wishing I could simply watch all day, however voyeuristic it seemed. Instead, I asked what I thought were simple questions with straightforward answers: How soon after the birth did she plan on going back to work? Did she have a nurse? But the explanations and details took hours. The other adults, I imagined, were taking the mental equivalent of cold showers to get babies off their minds. Then Roger poked his head in and said he thought it was time to leave.

The machine swung into motion again. The baby was burped, changed, and strapped into a contraption in the back seat of the car. "Bye, bye," they shouted, pulling away.

David, Marian, and I stood in the lobby, shocked by the quietness which suddenly enveloped us. "Did you spend any time with Roger?" Marian asked me.

Yes, for a moment Roger and I had found ourselves alone on Marian's patio, two old sweethearts who had known each other since we were practically babies ourselves. We didn't speak about our babies or anything else in the present or future tense. We reminisced about the junior high school French class we were in together, when he'd pass me notes with the lyrics of our favorite Beatles song: "I read the news today, oh boy."

"You two don't talk very much about the baby when you're together," Marian remarked that night after dinner. David and I were leaving in the morning; we'd see her next at the baby's birth.

"It's not the only thing in our lives," David said. "And we don't want to alienate everyone."

"Don't worry," Marian said, sounding bitter, inconsolable. "You couldn't sound like Ruth even if you tried." Something inside her wished we would all disappear and take our babies with us. "You won't be like them," she said again, tight-lipped at the kitchen table, her beer gone flat. But this time it sounded like a question, and David and I jumped in: "Oh no, we swear, never," a hundred times.

In my mailbox upon our return was an acceptance of an essay I had written for a magazine with national circulation, a magazine which my friends could pick up at any newsstand instead of depending on me to mail it to them. The enthusiastic note from the editor asked me to phone; she was generous with praise, asked me for more ideas, and invited me to lunch.

What a time for my career to get going. I sat at my desk, staring at my typewriter until the form of a baby appeared on the machine itself, dangling its little legs and crying for attention.

My father had foreseen this, I thought, remembering a conversation I had with him early in my pregnancy. Flushed with excitement which comes slow to him, he'd asked, "Now isn't this better than publishing a story?"

"It's just different," I had stammered. Having posed the same question to myself earlier didn't prevent me from getting angry at him. It was as if I had to pit parts of myself against each other, a task not only unfair but impossible. Anyone could get pregnant—ostriches, even ants have babies. Writing took skill, perseverance, vision. But perhaps what scared me the most was the thought that I too could confuse these achievements, taking the pride usually reserved for intellectual endeavors in the baby, letting the knowledge that I was pregnant cushion professional blows.

I had another phone call to make that afternoon, to my chairperson at the college where I was an adjunct instructor. Today was the last day I could inform her of any changes in my course scheduled for next February, one month after the baby's birth.

Everyone I had consulted urged me to take that semester off, telling me that I would be exhausted, that maternity leave was expected, essential. But I had heard of women who had returned to work after only a month or two, and if they could do it, why shouldn't I? Trying to focus on what I *felt* like doing didn't help at all because I had no idea of how I would feel. To try to presage my feelings seemed as ludicrous as trying to imagine myself a man.

I considered reducing my course load. This way, I could continue teaching, but face less pressure. I decided to try out this seemingly reasonable solution on my friend Gail, who had no children herself but lots of friends with kids. "Look," she said, "women more energetic than you are dripping with exhaustion. Call this number. Ask for Heidi. She has a four-month-old. See what she says."

I took the number but didn't phone. Instead, I called my chair, who was more understanding than I had imagined. "No problem," she said. "All I want from you is an announcement after the baby is born."

When I was weary, the fears that hadn't really vanished tiptoed out of their room, a blurry foreboding. So much for me as a stereotypic pregnant woman—sunny, fat, uncaring. Did she exist anywhere?

In my summer class was a young man of twenty-six crippled

by multiple sclerosis. Last week he had asked me to wheel him to the restaurant where he was to meet a friend, and I was amazed at my ineptitude pushing the wheelchair. To my apologies as I jostled him up and down curbs, he joked, "You'll soon have to do better than this." He had been healthy until four years ago. And so was my sister-in-law, the cancer that killed her at twenty-six a well-kept secret until nearly the end. A healthy baby could be programmed for disease at any future time. At what point would it not seem my responsibility? What diseases, problems, complications could I deal with? Bad eyesight. An extra earlobe. A missing finger. The list kept getting longer. There must be something I couldn't cope with. But what did it mean, not to cope?

Sometimes, thinking about my parents, I found myself beginning a statement like this: If they should die . . . Then I caught myself, for I knew the If must be changed to a When. I was doing the same thing with the baby. It wasn't an If something should go wrong, but only a When. Health, in the broadest sense, is not only relative but temporary.

My friend Randy was sleeping when I walked into her hospital room, but her mother ushered me into the best chair, tucked a pillow behind the small of my back, and slipped a plastic cup of apple juice into my hand. At first her ministrations and attention to my fatigue, thirst, weight gain, and mood embarrassed me; after all, Randy was the patient, recuperating from an emergency appendectomy. But the heatwave we were in exacted a real toll on me. My condition merited attention, my body as unstable as any patient's. Coming to the hospital helped me figure out where I fit in the continuum of health/ill health. Distinctions were blurring. Fetal growth rate is matched only by that of cancerous cells: early embryonic development is a kind of malignancy, a mad overreaction triggered by something we can't entirely discern.

This afternoon Randy wanted to go up to the hospital roof.

She took my arm for our slow walk to the elevator. The paleness of the convalescents made them almost transparent in the brilliant sun. They lounged on beach chairs, their tubes and paraphernalia tucked into department store shopping bags, donned sunglasses, rolled up the sleeves of their gowns; what a strange resort atop Central Park. Randy was quiet, so I studied the groves of children in the park playing softball, jumping rope, running, and the legion of women pushing carriages. I'll have a city baby, I thought to myself. Both Randy and I grew up in the suburbs where no one thought much about bodies except to shave or deodorize them. We didn't know then that bodies had minds of their own.

Randy soon tired and we returned to her room, but I found myself obsessed by the thought that soon I'd be in the hospital, perhaps subject to emergency surgery, the victim of a mutinous body. Me—disfigured? Scarred?

The elevator I rushed into headed up instead of down, and when the door opened I found myself staring into the corridor along which was housed the intensive care nursery. The shift was changing; jocular nurses and aides maneuvered the isolettes as unthinkingly as the cafeteria workers downstairs moved huge metal bins of dirty trays. I couldn't see the babies, but saw the tube holders and heard the machines. I suppose what finally shocked me the most was realizing that in the hospital, on any floor, you are always only someone's job.

David and I left the city in August, heading first to his parents' home in Hinsdale, Massachusetts. Sunny days found me bobbing on the float, waiting for motorboats to give me a ride, but August isn't the Berkshires' sunniest month. I spent hours watering the plants but couldn't garden, a task I'd always loved. It wasn't simply that lifting forkfuls of rocky soil was too strenuous, but exposing the underside of the earth, the pink worms and pale white roots, the buried, secret, furious life left me weak and mentally nauseated.

I, like the zucchini, had been growing since early spring, was tending my crop through the warm months to be delivered in the late, dark part of the year. This cosmic resonance, feeling absolutely in synch with nature, with summer, enervated more than enlivened me.

Each morning David positioned me in front of the bedroom mirror to assess the night's growth, front and side views, fit for a post office wall. "I feel as if I was only the soup starter," he lamented at breakfast, sounding very left out. The heftier I grew, the more his contribution, however essential to get things started, seemed overshadowed by current events.

We needed a fetal name. For weeks we had been trying to find one, but had come up with only goofy possibilities: Halyard, Mostly. One night, looking up from a book on fetal development, David said: "Lanugo." It was the vestigial body hair which covers a baby and is shed before birth, sometimes found behind the ears or in the baby's first waste. Lanugo was probably sprouting his lanugo right now.

David and I were very much on our raft that month, freely enjoying our idleness and closeness. We delighted in a letter from Gail, who, stuck in the city, wrote: "I took a walk with my friend's two-year-old daughter. The good news is that with a baby you're off limits. Entire rows of construction workers eating lunch let us pass without a titter. People who stop you ask only about the baby. She was intent on dropping stones down my dress so she could reach in and feel my titties. A ten-block walk took all afternoon. We had to admire everything. The stone. The pigeon. It was wonderful."

"I can't wait," I told David. A letter arrived from friends doing geographical fieldwork in the Sudan. "Imagine," I said, "children born outside of hospitals to mothers who don't read books and worry about their milk coming in." Wasn't there a lesson in all this?

If, I mused later that day, I opened up a savings account now and deposited ten dollars each week, Lanugo would have enough money after high school graduation to finance a trip to Europe or Israel or Africa. That's when I had to stop and laugh. How could I think that going for a stint on a kibbutz will be as romantic a notion in 2000 as it was in 1969, when everyone I knew with some extra bucks and lenient parents hopped on a plane and headed to Israel to pick peaches? Effortlessly I had slid into the trap of assuming that my child would want what I had wanted. Lanugo's world would be alien in many ways. After all, the raft David and I shared was entirely time-bound; we were stuck in our own generational rut.

Only here in the country was it possible to pretend, at least for a summer, that things were constant, that in eighteen more years this house would be pretty much the same, the lake cutting the same cove, the smoke bush we had planted during our first summer here still in its circle of wood chips. Parents would still be parents; we'd recite the same lines. Maybe one summer afternoon I'd knock on my son's bedroom door and walk in too quickly to find him on the couch necking (would they call it necking? making out?) and beat a hasty retreat, only to have my son say to me later, "You know, Mom, just because Roberta is five months pregnant doesn't mean we don't have an amorous relationship."

"I don't want to hear about it," I'd say. That's what my mother-in-law said, that was what mothers *always* said, right?

David and I rented a cabin in Eastham, Cape Cod, for a week with Randy and her boyfriend Frank. The cabin had two bedrooms and for a strange reason, an illicit air I hadn't experienced since college.

Sexuality permeated our little cabin; we went to bed early, woke up late, met furtively to and from the bathroom. All summer I had been caught short by how sexual I felt, and here I couldn't help but confront it. The pleasure of no birth control was only part of the story. So were hormones. I was in a nearly continual state of excitement, wanting to make love every day, several times a day and at odd hours, like a kid.

Even the anorexic model of beauty to which I had aspired all my life was mysteriously being replaced by a new one. I eyed the eighteen-year-old girls on the beach coolly. Sure, they were sexy, bronze and taut, strutting around in bathing suits cut skimpy on top and high on the leg. But so was I. I had my fullness, my heft, which I was actually beginning to enjoy flaunting.

What David enjoyed was that I no longer placed my cold feet against his, that the baby raised my temperature and transformed me into someone who was warm and cuddly. Yet as willing and loving a partner as he was that summer, I knew that my bulk interested him only as a change, an oddity; that he missed my old body. He waged a brave one-man campaign to debunk the popular myth that pregnant women are lovelier than ever. It was a tricky position to maintain—to keep me from feeling rejected while assuring me that he loved and enjoyed the old me. "It's postsexual, in a way," he explained one afternoon as we walked on the beach. "We've already accomplished what sex accomplishes." So this was sex in a new key. We both chuckled about the latest surprise of pregnancy: my horniness.

We didn't spend all our time in bed, of course; the vacation progressed as vacations do, though it too was different. In the past I'd plan a full week of ambitious activities, and feel scorn for those who couldn't match my energy. Now, I was often the weakest of our quartet, the most in need of a break or a drink. Frank went off alone on the best hike the Cape had to offer, a ten-miler out on a peninsula in the middle of the bay, while Randy, David, and I accompanied old people and families with young children on a boardwalk built through a pine forest. We did go to the cranberry bogs at my instigation, but once there I identified most with a ten-year-old who kept pulling on his father's sleeve and whining, "Let's go home. It's hot."

One night, while the men were out shopping, Randy knocked on my door and walked in before I could slip back into my shirt. I'd been examining my breasts in the mirror. "It's okay," I told her, though self-conscious and unsure why; I used to think nothing of being naked in front of my women friends. "Look at all these things," I said—the blemishes, discolorations, and warts that had begun appearing on my face, breasts, torso. The doctor had assured me these would go away but I didn't believe her.

"What about this?" Randy said, pulling down her pants to reveal her fresh scar. It looked raw, unalterable. The room began to feel like a college dorm room, but we were far from naively believing, as we did when we were coeds, that a stable personality rests inside a body subject to erosions and disfigurements of all kinds. Physical changes work inward, and alter how we think of ourselves. I'd never return to the svelte young thing I was before, no matter how much weight I lost; Randy's scar would never disappear.

"What's happening to us?" she cried. She sounded outraged, as if demanding of a conductor whether the ticket she had purchased didn't have another destination.

Back in Hillsdale, with Labor Day so close, I decided to do what I had wanted to do since our first Berkshire summer—take the canoe out alone. The baby still hadn't kicked and I needed to work out the implications of this by myself.

I had no problem steering the big aluminum Lincoln canoe into the middle of the lake, where I sunned for a while, drifted, admired water skiers. But when I tried to return home, wind and water turned against me. So powerless was I to maneuver the canoe that I wondered if I hadn't forgotten how to paddle. As if in a whirlpool, I'd progress a few strokes but end up in the same cove, directly opposite our dock. I began to feel invisible; boaters and skiers who only five minutes ago had waved now had no idea of my predicament. I recalled a spill I had taken as a child on ice skates. With the wind knocked out of me, I sat on my bottom and thought, I am going to die right here with all these people circling around me, even my own father. That same moment of childish panic swept over me now, weakening me further. "I'll never get home," I began repeating to myself, "never. Not until David gets home from town, then he'll ask for me, only then it will be dark and they'll light lanterns and tow me . . ."

Then I noticed that the wind had died down, and paddled in a frenzy back to our cove, where my anxious father-in-law hauled me in. I limped out of the canoe and collapsed.

That night I was in bed much earlier than usual, working covertly on the baby quilt which I wasn't supposed to touch until I felt the baby move. I had assembled the precut squares, sewn the long double seams, and was now adding the borders by hand, unable to wait until I got home to use the machine. I felt something on my right side, not a kick or a thud or a flutter, nothing I could describe to anyone, nothing that the books had described. If David were next to me I probably would have said, "Guess what?" and this would have been the moment forever inscribed in our memory as Lanugo's first word. But David was in the shower. He liked long showers, which meant I would have to get up and tell him, or stay awake until he came inside. Then he would be full of questions: Are you sure? What did it feel like? Where did you feel it? For how long? I was too tired to answer. So I shut the light and said nothing. I knew it was Lanugo but I figured his first communication was for my ears only: Hey. Take it easy. What were you trying to prove out there on the lake? Think about me, too.

We celebrated the end of summer at the Williamstown Theatre Festival's production of Noël Coward's *Nude with Violin*. We sat on folding chairs in the back of the auditorium and in the middle of Act II, I felt something unmistakable—a thump. I nudged David. "I feel him," I said. "Lanugo, right here." I put his hand over my now still stomach. He looked at me, then at his mother on his right, and for a moment I thought he was going to lean over to her and say "The baby kicked," as if we were playing telephone. Instead, he squeezed my hand, turned back to the play, and kept his hand on my stomach waiting for an encore. But having exerted himself that much, Lanugo went back to sleep for a couple of days.

Marian's younger brother Paul chose Labor Day weekend and the Princeton University Faculty Club for his wedding. The building had a marble staircase leading to a portico and formal gardens where the ceremony took place. An old college boyfriend arrived soon after David and I did with his date, a young, divorced woman who worked full time, went to school, and had a six-year-old daughter.

She wore, as did most of the other women, a silky dress with tight waist and graceful lines. Marian looked striking in a red floral dress and high heels. I wore a borrowed gray and pink tent and sensible pumps.

Watching the ceremony, it struck me what elaborate games of rearrangement rituals are. Two people declare their love and those surrounding them receive new names, new roles. So too with a birth.

Marian's grandmother, whom I have known since I was twelve, was the last on the official receiving line. I offered her a kiss and congratulations. She told me how lovely I looked, took my hands, and said, "I hope you have a happy, healthy baby and when he grows up you make him a beautiful wedding like this."

I smiled and she said, "Oh listen to me, he's not even born and I'm marrying him off." I assured her it was all right. For some reason I felt a special kind of kinship with her, much more than I did with the young woman who, after hours of feasting and dancing, caught the bride's bouquet.

4

The Third Trimester
Lanugo

"A s you can see," I announced to my writing class, "I'm pregnant." The third trimester and the fall term began simultaneously. David and I were back in the city working, seeing friends, dreaming.

"They don't mind that you teach?" asked one anxious aunt. I refused to acknowledge her question—how could anyone mind that? But privately I felt a twinge of unsightliness under the scrutiny of twenty-five pairs of eighteen-year-old eyes; some smiled, some looked away.

I directed my students' attention to the syllabus, a comforting week-by-week reckoning of the semester. Simply fulfill these requirements in this much time, it states, and you will pass. I appreciated its clarity, the academic rhythm familiar and reliable: midterms, pre- and post-vacation weeks, finals. On my own copy I had numbered the weeks ahead according to the medical signposts, and also counted backward from my due date so I could tell at a glance how much time was left. Doctor's visits, which resumed at their monthly rate only to accelerate at the end, were also penciled in. Timetables began overlapping, activities crowding each other—Lamaze classes, the hospital visit, my baby shower.

And saturating each day's progress was my sense of the natural calendar, the year speeding toward its end as if from its own accumulated weight, as I rushed headlong into the tunnel of Thanksgiving, Christmas, New Year's, then ten more days till blastoff.

Many students came up after class to tell me about their niece, their friend's baby, their cousin's pregnancy. One woman waited for all the others to leave. "When are you due?"

"Right around the time of your final."

"Oh," she said. "Could you try and wait until after our test?"

Lanugo, no longer a shadowy presence, happily indulged me that semester, allowing me energy and eagerness to work, swim, walk, take buses, and socialize. I was proud of the bulge that showed through my most tentlike jumpers, and even bought a pretty party dress. Yet what most characterized this phase was the profusion of my dreams, complete little plays produced and staged by someone I didn't know but who knew everything about me.

I am explaining to my mother how nervous I am about the baby's development. She looks puzzled; asks, "Don't you know?" She places me on my back, raises my knees, and scoops out of my vagina, as if it were an oven, a tiny trussed chicken dusted with paprika. "See?" she asks, as if to say, This is all you have to do. I am completely relieved to see a healthy baby. My mother gently shoves it back in; it's browning nicely, but not quite ready.

My parents and I talked incessantly about physically accommodating the baby: where to move furniture; which room to make into the nursery; what baby furniture to buy. David had no part of this. He and his mother remained suspicious and firmly opposed to advance planning. While my mother and I knitted sweater and bonnet sets in neutral yellows and greens, my mother-in-law contented herself by spinning verbal equivalents: "The first child is for the grandparents," she'd say, "the second for the father, and the third for the mother."

One day my parents and I left David at home and drove to a children's store. "This is where I got toys for you and your sister," my father said, swinging into the parking lot. Wait a second—*those* toys, precious readers and activity books, Fascination by Remco—came from a store, purchased with money? How could they have had such a pedestrian origin as this wall-to-ceiling toybox, full of greedy, glassy-eyed kids and tired, acquiescent adults?

What were we doing here? We looked as suspicious as shop-lifters, stalking the aisles with our glazed expressions, our timing off (we were way too early), hoping no one would notice. "Let's go," I said, surreptitiously checking the price tags on my way out so that when David asked if I saw anything I could say, noncha-lantly, "It's all so expensive."

"Don't worry, darling," my grandmother said from her hospi-tal bed. "I'll give you a check. Everything's on Grandma." She was hooked to a device that monitored her heart twenty-four hours a day. I told her that babies about to be born are monitored like this. She clasped my hand. Her wink said, "Listen, fifty-five years ago when I was in labor they did no such thing." "You'll have to cut your nails to pick up the baby," she said. "And get your husband to help you with the housework. It's no shame."

"Your mother always kept you so clean," she went on, babies now stuck in her mind, "spotless." I had heard this before and it always bothered me, proclaimed as if that were the best one could do for an infant. But tonight it brought other memories: of our old toybox, the top of my dresser, my sister's Bathinette with its neat provisions—Q-tips, powder, baby oil. I saw us bathed and sham-pooed, hair combed and wet, sitting on the couch in front of the TV, munching cheese sliced into squares. It was summer, a warm evening; we were both wearing red and white seersucker pajamas and red slippers; it was still light outside.

One evening, after dinner out with my parents, my mother slipped her arm into mine to say, "Slow down." David and my father walked on ahead. She wanted to make sure I knew that in the seventh month a woman should stop having intercourse. It had been twenty-five years since she received this advice. And I shouldn't resume sex until after my first period. I told her, gently, that my doctor advised me to have sex as long as I wanted, and that I could resume six weeks after birth, period or no. She took this news, along with my remark that sex may be a good, natural way to induce labor, with equanimity, as if to say, "My, how things have changed." I wondered how her thoughts were running, if she was even a little angry at the misinformation she had been fed. Imagine, women of her generation having sex proscribed for five or six months. I'm sure there were and are women who would welcome such a long period of release from marital relations, but I couldn't tell from her placid, absent expression whether she was one who did, whether she felt unduly victimized in retrospect, or whether I was feeding her ammunition she didn't want.

"Families," I said later to David, relating her conversation, those hotbeds of feelings, both the spoken and unspoken, the undeniable closeness, whatever the emotion. I will be to my child what my parents are to me, that which cannot be shaken off or silenced—only muted and then most often unsuccessfully. My child's partner for this unending tango will be *me*, children and parents the only dancers, grandparents remote spectators. And my sister, whom I sat next to, whispered to on sultry nights when we couldn't sleep, fought with and ignored, our family's baby, will be my baby's aunt. New names will have to be forged. "I don't want to be called Nannie," my mother warned.

I am on the gray sofa in the apartment in which I grew up, playing with my baby, a girl with pale red hair and perfect skin. She is naked. I touch her cheeks and say, "Apple cheeks." She burbles and coos but then repeats, clearly, "Apple cheeks." I rush her over to David, but she won't say it for him, only me.

Not every dream unfolded at night behind closed eyes. One evening, as David cooked dinner, I was on my back hammering curtain rods into the French doors I had refinished last spring.

In the living room Lanugo looks up from a book to say, "Gee, Mom and Dad, you certainly are great about breaking the myth of sexual stereotypes."

David served the chicken and vegetables from the wok and noted that our dinners together were numbered. But the meals weren't nearly as precious as the mornings which we'd also lose, when we woke up early and stayed in bed just to talk. This was more than shared time; it prepared me for the day, gave me a protective coating which I sorely missed on days when we had to get up quickly.

With fewer than twenty weeks to go, I was slowly realizing that the finely tuned life David and I had evolved together was on the verge of extinction. The date we had so long been focused on would indeed end the pregnancy and all the adjustments we'd had to make, but how could we have deluded ourselves into thinking we could then step out for a moment, recalibrate, reacquaint ourselves with our own familiar kinesthetics both alone and together? We'd go from advanced pregnancy to immediate parenthood; we'd already be in the throes of our exotic, overwhelming new life before we'd remember that we hadn't joined hands and closed our eyes before jumping.

I no longer cared how much the scale at Dr. Peters's office inched up; daily ice cream was as much a part of my routine as coming home, shedding my clothes, putting my feet up, and remarking to David how many more women than men offered me seats on buses and trains. At a faculty meeting, my chair said, "Make way for the big lady," as I negotiated a seat; a student offered me a magazine article with beauty tips during pregnancy.

"You look good with some weight," the doctor told me.

"For now," I said. "What about after the birth?"

"American women, all the same. It will all come off, all in a snap, except what you gained the first few months. That you need. You were too skinny." She patted my belly and I felt like a corpulent executive after a big meal, admiring his bulging stomach for the extra leverage it gave him.

But now it wasn't only a question of weight. I was providing room for Lanugo who needed it. He tumbled in his capsule so deftly and constantly that Dr. Peters had trouble pinning him down to find his heart. "Who's in there?" I kept asking myself, as if I were a video game.

He was like a prizefighter before a fight, a family of ten stuck in two rooms. One night he erupted in a meteor shower of activity distending my stomach enough for David to witness. It wasn't a pleasant sensation as sensations go, the way the baby swooped, kicked, bounced off the trampoline of my pelvic floor, but because it was all a signal to me I cherished each tremor. Eventually, I could predict and plot his movements, the peaks, stillnesses, the arcs of his curves as he rose to the top of his trajectory, sounded and dove back to the bottom, a student of the whales we had seen from a boat in Provincetown a month ago.

One night he stayed awake for an entire World Series game, a frolicking, soundless creature who could only speak by crashing his furry body into mine, who was exercising his new toothpick limbs, moving on his own—such a big Lanugo. I'd miss feeling him. This pregnancy was our one moment of unity, everything that would follow a long, inexorable, often painful separation. At the instant he or she was affixed a name, Lanugo would be obscured, overshadowed by the person he became. He had reality now—we communicated, coexisted. I knew friends who would quake to hear me; I was setting back the cause of abortion fifteen years by maintaining I already had a child. But I did. And I would lose him, as he existed now, the moment he was born.

I see the baby's foot sticking out of my stomach, so I grab it and pull. By the time David comes the whole baby is out, big and clean—a boy with closed eyes. But as soon as he opens his eyes he begins talking

and then he becomes David's sister Laura, talking about her boyfriend.
I feel terribly cheated. I had no labor, no pain, no chance to take part
in his birth. My baby already exists in the world no thanks to me.

September's visit to Dr. Peters went smoothly. I met a woman in
the waiting room with information about discount maternity
clothes. We were exchanging fashion tips when the door opened
and a woman entered literally holding up her belly—something so
huge that it looked as if it couldn't belong to her, but was only stuck
on by some sick joke of anatomy. She was dressed as if for the
theatre in a white linen suit, low black pumps, even stockings, and
her diminutive husband darted behind her, adjusting her shoulder
bag, steering her by the elbow. She walked directly to the reception
desk, barely fitting through the door, and after some behind-the-
scenes scurrying about we in the waiting room heard nothing. A
moment later the receptionist made a call, explaining that a woman
had just gone into labor in the office. They took her out the side
door to the hospital. My companion and I exchanged stricken
looks. "I know exactly what you're thinking," she said. "How
could that ever happen to *us?*"

That afternoon I baked bread. Standing beside me was
Lanugo, kneading a tiny loaf, pressing it into a toy pan. My mother
used to let me bake with her, and I made unnaturally colored cakes
for my father which we always set on his dinner plate. How had
he managed to convince me it was delicious without actually touching it to his lips?

My stomach interfered with the kneading, a terribly winding
activity, like the swims I took only a few times a week now. Lanugo
had begun his journey. He wasn't so internal any more, but was
moving out into my belly where he was more apparent and vulnerable, more in the world. The skin over my belly felt as thin as the
membrane under an eggshell. Light reached him in there, as did
sound.

My little space traveler, jostled by my work, do you hear the song I'm singing to you? My heartbeat? The rush of my blood? How will you like our world, baby astronaut in your tiny space-ship which, by some miraculous calculation, landed inside of me?

I go to the bathroom in the morning and find that I have my period. I have always known that this pregnancy is a dream. I look down, my belly is flat, I am skinny again. Struggling to wake up, I find my hand on my belly—still huge, still here.

The twenty-eighth week, we learned, was when a fetus became "viable." The term came from Sue, a friend who was a gynecologist-obstetrician. When she described babies born at this point, she smiled, as if to spare the details: "Chickens you eat are bigger."

At our October visit to Dr. Peters, we saw a movie in her waiting room about a woman's labor and delivery. David and I chuckled through it—the seriousness, the amateurish quality. But at the end, when the baby's head popped out, we were both surprised to find that we were in tears. Mine weren't only for the baby, but for the mother too. She'd done it! And what about me? How would I hold up, how good a performance would I give? I shunned the spotlight; I craved it.

My examination went well. The doctor asked what I was doing right to keep my hemoglobin count so high, and promised that the calcium pills would take care of my leg cramps at night. As I dressed in the tiny bathroom, wondering if next month I'd even fit inside, I heard Dr. Peters cut through David's stammerings: "Yes, yes, week twenty-eight, the baby will survive now. Viable, yes. Tell me, why are you so worried?"

Dr. Peters isn't prepared for me. She is naked under her white coat, she has lost her glasses, her nurse is frazzled. They forget to take my urine or blood, to weigh me, they hurry me through the exam. When I complain about the pressure under my rib, Dr. Peters kneels down to give me mouth-to-mouth resuscitation. It is sexual, erotic. But when

I go into her office, a strange doctor sits behind her desk. Dr. Peters is gone . . .

Forty people, all paired off except for me, trooped through Women's Hospital on our official tour. We gathered on the labor and delivery floor, which was freezing, deserted, and resonating with an eerie, amplified pulse as if we weren't inside a hospital but the human body itself. "What is that sound?" we asked each other.

Our guide quieted us in front of a huge blackboard, noting patient name and status, and staff whereabouts. "What you hear," she said slowly—the tour was replete with stragglers and loud-mouths—"is a fetal heart monitor." A nurse wearing a shower cap wheeled one over for our inspection. "Some doctors use them, some don't," our guide said. "Be sure you know what yours intends."

Only one woman was in labor tonight, and we avoided looking into her room, though the contents could be taken in at a glance: huge clock, metal chair, stretcher. Monastic wasn't the word.

"We also have two birthing rooms," our guide added; these had floral curtains, a padded chair, and a bedspread—motel décor. The rooms were assigned on a first-come, first-served basis and only to those with no complications.

Next we donned gowns and masks and were permitted, two by two, into the delivery room, a cold, metal room of torturous devices, a room like a steel inquisition chamber.

"It sure doesn't look like hospitals on TV," I said to the woman next to me.

"Oh, this is a good hospital," she said. "They have good food." We were downstairs now, looking at patient rooms which were cozied up to seem like resorts in comparison. At the nursery we peered through venetian blinds at the new babies. One, just born, was on his back in a plastic crib under a heater, kicking and stretching. Hey, I know those movements, I thought, that's what Lanugo does.

Until now I had thought of birth as a moment of crystallization: the soft, unwrapped, gelatinous babyflesh coalescing the moment it hit air, skin forming instantly, seamlessly with the change of medium. Now I saw that babies were finished inside and came as if swallowed whole. The thought of Lanugo's skin, of his entirety inside me, spooked me.

The world too new a place to sleep in, this baby sunbathed on his back, refusing to succumb despite heavy eyelids. He looked the way I had arriving in Paris. So *this* is it? Amused, to have expected something so different; helpless, to feel so misplaced. So this is *it?*

Many on the tour shied away from the premature nursery, but I took a long, slow look. Nearest to the window was a tiny one, all wired up, looking perfectly formed but with no fat, the skin around the joints sagging rather than plump. As if my grandmother had been taken from her hospital bed and shrunk.

Downstairs, we were briefed on what to bring to the hospital, what not to bring, which entrance to use at which time, and advised to avoid coming before midnight if possible so we wouldn't be billed for the entire previous day. We were exhorted to be adamant about letting the nurses know our demands: did we want to nurse at two in the morning; was sugar water permissible; which formula would we prefer. Without constant vigilance, it seemed, things could slip out of control. I tried to remember everything our guide said since I had forgotten to bring a pencil, but my head became clogged as if refusing to absorb simple information. No information was simple any more, everything required attention, evaluation, decisions. I borrowed a pen and scribbled notes on a scrap of paper from the floor. I couldn't have come more unprepared. I'd even let David attend his class.

"Movie time," our guide said. This one was about a Lamaze class composed of six women of different socioeconomic and ethnic backgrounds, all with minor but complicating wrenches thrown into their deliveries. I cried at each birth. Delivering a baby, it seemed, was a cross between two otherwise discrete bodily functions—an excretion of a profoundly orgasmic nature.

I assumed this wasn't what our guide had in mind when she raised the lights and asked if there were any questions or comments. I'd missed David all night, but never more than now.

He was hungry for details when I returned, but the tour had left me with complex impressions rather than concrete, factual information to impart. I'd seen, for example, that mother and child weren't the only ones who bonded during birth. Husbands and wives bonded to each other in their new roles as parents.

I'd seen too that I'd have to stop thinking of myself in labor in the passive voice. Labor wasn't so much something that would happen to me as something over which I could exert some control, if only in my attitude. I had to swear off the belief, rampant in my family, that things go wrong unless you're exceptionally lucky. If I was the star, I could also, to some extent, direct.

"Just stay in control," my midwestern friend had told me. "Stay on top of things, don't panic and lose the rhythm."

My friend Beth had disagreed. "If I were going to have a child"—she knew she never would—"I'd let it all out. All thirty years' worth. It's the only time you're allowed to, your only chance —hell, I'd scream my brains out."

"Did you meet anyone interesting?" David asked. We were sleepily getting ready for bed. I had walked home with a nice couple who lived just a block away, who were expecting a day before we were. "Did you get their number?" he asked. It was in my coat pocket. But I knew I'd never call. Someone else's unfinished story was the last thing I wanted to hear.

Through a pinhole in my eyeglasses I see myself in the middle of an ocean on a boat. I need rescue. A woman on shore, a ship's commander, tells me to hold my breath and then I'll float. I can't. I begin to moan. She rides out on a bicycle/baby carriage and the water turns to sand. "Now isn't this easy," she says, leading me back to shore and back through the tiny, ever-regressing hole . . .

Week 30: the pregnancy three-fourths over. I still wanted the time to go quickly but only through force of habit. Suddenly having only ten weeks left of life as we knew it seemed much too little. "The next time you'll be alone together," said our downstairs neighbor Nan, mother of eighteen-month-old Leah, "is when you drive your kid to college." David and I would be in our late forties, at the start of a new century. I remembered when my parents turned what sounded like an ancient thirty-five. Nan and her husband were now thirty-four—young, energetic, as unparental as I felt.

If I timed my mornings right, I'd meet Nan and Leah on their daily stroll. Each day Leah recited new words: *peacock, elevator, macaroni*—every syllable an entire poem. I couldn't get enough of her.

"You're doing great," Nan said, confessing that she and her husband were hugely depressed in the last months of her pregnancy, unable to work or concentrate. "It was as rough a period as my first trimester," she said. I wanted to hug her—my first soulmate. "Please, tell me everything."

"I can hardly remember being pregnant," she said. "All the vague fears evaporated once Leah was home and we had to deal with her reality." There was no end to good news. Soon all this would be over and in its place a beautiful, winning child like Leah . . .

Nan thanked me for each compliment I offered, but shook her

head impatiently as if I were missing the point. "Pregnancy is the *easy* part," she said.

"I want a baby who's wide-eyed," I told David that night, thinking of Leah, her lips wrapped around her newly minted words.

"We'll take what we get," he said.

Our Lamaze class began during my thirty-second week. When it ended, we'd be days away from Christmas. Things were finally getting exciting.

A rollicking class was in progress when David and I arrived. Like an elephant on tiptoes, I skirted the couples sprawled on the plush carpeting, reclining on pillows, laughing in enviable camaraderie. Anatomical pictures in soft pinks and yellows lined the walls, a bulletin board displayed a raggedy collage of baby pictures and birth announcements.

Our class—eight couples—assembled in the cramped hallway, the women looking like bumper cars as we attempted to take off our shoes, hang our coats, affix name tags. Each was fussily attended by a husband who seemed dwarfed, reduced to abashed helpfulness, positioning chairs and cushions. The tags and no shoes were touches designed to put us at ease, but they seemed to have the reverse effect.

Our teacher, a young woman with curly red hair, asked us to "share" our names, professions, and why we had opted for the Lamaze technique. As we recited our statistics, I realized that we all sounded hesitant, withdrawn. This wasn't the way it was supposed to be, certainly not the way it was in the movies. But everything around us which conspired to make us feel intimate seemed forced, heavy-handed. We left feeling mutually suspicious.

Our teacher continued during the next six weeks to ask the

questions which should have helped us achieve group cohesion. One evening, she leaned forward in her seat, signaling that this was a heart-to-heart girl-talk. "What," she asked, "is the part of your pregnancy you hate the most?"

"Throwing up every day," one woman replied immediately.

"Anyone else?" our teacher asked, after a pause which indicated her distaste for such vivid realism. She sounded now like a pushy late night TV talk show host.

I mentioned the degree of physical limitation I experienced. One woman complained about leg cramps which virtually crippled her. And then one woman from the back of the room said, "Maternity clothes. You can't get maternity clothes in natural fibers. Everything's polyester."

I suppose we weren't an easy group to lead. But in fact the entire Lamaze approach proved enigmatic. Its rationale was logical enough: A woman's entire musculature need not go into contractions along with her uterus. To master this, we practiced relaxing one set of muscles while tensing others. And to help disengage the mind from uterine activity, we were given something completely arbitrary on which to concentrate—an artificial pattern of breathing.

Three patterns, or schedules, of in- and exhalations were developed, one to correspond to each of labor's three stages. Our husbands, true coaches with watches in hand, timed us and coaxed us through. Once they were instructed to pinch us hard, on the thigh, while we were focused on our breathing. Many of us reported, successfully, feeling the pain in a remote key.

But if learning to manage labor was like learning to drive a car with a manual transmission, a series of successive, accelerating gear shifts, then all Lamaze could offer was a dummy car on which to practice. We all also knew that every labor is as individual as a thumbprint, and that the course of labor according to which we learned our cues was a prototype, and only of limited usefulness.

The actual skills we had to learn could have been imparted in half the time. For the balance of the course we kept busy. We studied diagrams, learned facts, saw movies, even planned a reunion for March, an eternity away. We were supposed to ready our belongings for the hospital and most important, urged to practice the breathing at home. I welcomed the diversion. But I also couldn't stop thinking: Is this all I'll have to get me through?

Leah's father comes to visit. He brings a book of his daughter's development to date, and asks my sister and me to look at it with him. He begins slowly but soon turns the pages much too quickly. "Slow down," I beg him, frantic, and he's upset too but he can't stop, can't slow down the pages . . .

Pregnancy, increasingly a state of mind, was taking its toll. I was tired of the pep rallies I had to mentally stage each day. All this optimism didn't come naturally to me. Frankly, I was running out of steam. I worried about everything that worrying makes worse: my milk coming in, mother–infant bonding. Will mother nature take me under her wing? When I heard that a friend's friend delivered a baby boy after only two hours of labor, I said to myself, "That's it. She used up all the good luck."

After my C-section, I am walking around the hospital, my belly flattening, and I mean to call the nursery and see that my baby is okay. Then I meet a woman from my Lamaze class and her doctor. "She gave birth today," the doctor says proudly, "what a session we had, what a fighter she is." I am envious, angry. "Did you see your baby yet?" the woman asks. "No, not yet," I stammer, "I am just on my way . . ." They look at me with disbelief.

When I stood for too long my ankles and calves hurt, but sitting I felt a wincing pain under my left breast. One night, poking around for the source of the pain, I wrapped my fingers around one of the baby's limbs—right under my fingertips. I screamed, "I feel him," to David. I was thrilled and repelled—something alive inside me, in my most inviolate space, a membrane away.

That night Lanugo began an earthquake of movements that not only woke me but nearly drove me crazy. He roamed high and low, pummeling his little fists: Let me out of here. In desperation I began talking to myself, to Lanugo, assuring him that his assertiveness was wonderful to behold, that I wanted nothing more but that he grow strong, grow well. But you also have to let me sleep. I need strength too. I said this calmly, quietly, and gradually Lanugo dropped sweetly off to sleep.

I deliver the baby myself in the tiny foyer between our bedroom and bathroom. David plays the guitar nearby and I hear but don't see him. A girl slides out, effortlessly, all lubricated with vernix. I have no pain. We begin breast-feeding immediately. My mother is in the kitchen and I take my daughter in to see her.

Many out-of-town friends home for the holidays called and came to visit—as David said, "Last chance to see the big lady." Mark, the man I dated before meeting David, met me for tea. We were crossing Broadway when he said, "Benjamin, right?" I stopped in the middle of the street.

"How did you know?"

"You always said you'd name your son Benjamin," he said. I didn't remember anything of the sort. He had a bit more trouble with the girl's name; it took him two guesses to get to Sarah.

My baby shower took place on a blustery Sunday afternoon at Gail's apartment. Surprise guests included my sister, my friend Ann from Michigan with her nine-month-old daughter, and

Marian from Washington. After an elegant lunch of watercress sandwiches, crudités, and homemade casseroles, I was deposited in the most comfortable chair next to a vase of fresh flowers, a bottle of champagne, and a layer cake wishing me well. I opened all the presents. Marian took pictures and then made a toast. The best everyone had to offer was given to me and I tried to make myself acknowledge it, not grow shy and turn away. This was all for me and my baby, my unknown child.

Ann and her daughter had time before their flight home so they came back with me. The baby was sneezing, needed immediate changing, feeding. I tried to help but the cereal I made had the wrong consistency, the cup too much milk. Ann was patient with my ineptitude. Where had she learned all this? Did she remember that she had once not known it? The baby, tossing in her mother's arms, had long ago stopped being cute. Ann stuffed her into a snowsuit and then into an infant seat, and finally they rushed out to find a taxi.

Good riddance, I said after they were gone, this is too much reality too soon. Leave me my image of the baby I would have who never caught cold, spit up, cried, squirmed, or made a mother nervous.

For the rest of the evening I took refuge in the shower gifts, placing the stuffed animals on top of the dresser I had oiled, the clothes in the drawers I had lined. David came in to see. "Doesn't it look like an oversized jewelry box?" I asked him, the dresser neatly miniaturized. He nodded and left the room. We had both seen the news story last year about parents with a perfectly stocked nursery waiting for a baby to come; perhaps the next time wouldn't be a stillbirth.

A week later I purchased the layette: undershirts, robes, gowns, towels, washcloths, everything in combed cotton and gentle pastel colors, scores of tiny things I couldn't stop fingering, the piles made and unmade a hundred times a night. I draped them over my stomach, cradled them in my arms, imagined a head here, feet there. David even stopped trying to stop me.

My thirty-eighth-week visit to Dr. Peters was the first which left me more upset than assuaged. Even though all signs were fine— low blood pressure, strong heartbeat, small weight gain—I had an uneasy premonition. I asked her about having sex. "Is okay," she said, "as long as you feel like it. But nothing too violent. Just to please husband. Don't get too involved."

I thought she was finished with me but she handed me a piece of paper. "I want you to have sonogram again," she said, sneaking it in as if she hoped I wouldn't notice. I assumed that the baby hadn't yet turned over, but when I opened the form on the street I saw she had written, under the directions to the radiologist, "Anomalies?"

Sue, my gynecologist friend, tried to assure us that this was routine, but we sweated out the three days until the test, our long-buried fears bursting out of their hibernation. The radiologist, remembering us from the last time, said, "Again? What's up?"

"You tell us," I said, positioning myself on his cold, cold table.

"Everything looks okay," he said, "head right where it belongs."

"You mean we're engaged?" David asked.

"Engaged? I thought you were married." The doctor liked his joke. In great humor, he took us on a tour of the whole baby—arms, legs, body, midline of the brain, internal organs—everything intact. I asked if he could tell the sex.

"Only if you're sure you want to know." In that split second I knew I didn't. But then he told me that he couldn't tell for sure. He kept probing, all sides, all angles, until David asked if the ultrasound couldn't hurt the baby.

"Relax," the doctor said. "He's more nervous than anyone I've seen."

"Not more nervous, just more verbal," I said. The doctor's good mood was contagious. "Does the baby have curly hair?" I asked.

"Can't tell curls for sure, but that hair is very blond."

"Are you absolutely relieved?" David asked me on our way home, the pictures of the baby, a moon chart, emblazoned in both our minds. "Yes," I said. The baby was the right size for his age, the due date was confirmed. I waited for him to ask me if I saw any webbing between the fingers, a sign of possible retardation. David was master of exotic abnormalities—could it be that I knew one he didn't? His concern, about head size, seemed allayed. I kept my unasked question about webbing to myself; David had enough to worry about.

Armed with our good news, we went to a party one Saturday night at which we spent more time than we cared to talking with the other guests, most of whom were our age, childless, and professionals, about the baby and my condition. I felt like everyone's mother, a walking reminder that no one was getting any younger. We had to leave early, one reality of my condition which made David unhappy. On the way home, we began speaking about the need he foresaw for us to preserve a sense of ourselves as individuals, as a couple, and as a trio. "We'll have to learn to relate as three from scratch," he said, but he was afraid that this would overshadow our oneness and twoness. Mostly he worried about having time for himself, whereas I was concerned that we'd have no time to be together, just us.

He assured me that he wouldn't press his need to be alone if it hurt me, and I told him I could get through most anything as long as he could reassure me, verbally, of his commitment to me. It was nearly midnight, gusty and cold; we walked close together and quickly, the wind whipping off the hills of Riverside Park and tunneling up West 116th Street, past the dorms of Barnard College where I had lived more years ago than I cared to calculate, an ignorant coed dying for her life to begin.

Our talk, taking care of the last piece of business we had to deal with, freed me to begin the modern-day equivalent of confinement. I still did what I had to do—taught, socialized—but my soul took to bed. This was the last block of time I'd have to myself ever, I thought; I had to take advantage of it. I stopped thinking of what I should do and did more of what I wanted to. If that meant cleaning out closets, fine; if my need to clean was a vestigial nesting instinct, that was fine too. Confinement at this late date in the pregnancy and year sounded like a good idea—I had already slipped on the street once; it was cold and dark outside; I was most comfortable lying down. I made my way leisurely through baby care books, reading slowly about how to hold the baby, how to bathe him, until the anxiety each new task elicited dissipated. If I read too far ahead I'd grow sleepy, all that information too much to absorb. I'd take my time.

David brought news from the outside world, and told me the story of his little sister's homecoming when he was twelve. His parents placed the baby in the middle of their bed, and the whole neighborhood came to admire her, forming a human crib around this magic, moving thing. David had recently dreamed that he held our baby at the window of his old bedroom to show her his back-yard, the clothesline, the basketball hoops, the steps to the stores and the world beyond.

"It could be any day," I told him. "Can you imagine me saying at any moment, 'I feel it'?" Soon, I pleaded, soon.

"No." Then he had a question for me. "If you could have it tomorrow, would you?"

"No," I said. "Not tomorrow."

. . .

My sexual energy evaporated as mysteriously and suddenly as it had overtaken me. It was as if a valve in my brain simply closed and shunted those juices elsewhere. David was very understanding; in the past weeks sex had been more engineering than rapture as we struggled to negotiate my enormous mass. "We'll figure something out," he assured me. "Don't worry."

He came home with a new hairbrush and each night before dinner he brushed my hair up off my neck, exposing its silkiest side, reminding me that I had graceful curves still, if only on my nape. We took naked pictures of me with a Polaroid camera intended as a baby gift. We slipped them into a tiny photo album and stuck them in the top of our dresser, our time capsule. And then it was New Year's Eve.

"Not even a *sip?*" I was asked over and over that night, at the dinner party we went to, and then the dance party. Champagne didn't tempt me. I hoped for a comfortable seat ("You looked like an old grandma parked on the couch," David told me later, laughing, until he saw that I was near tears—what else could I do?) and prayed that the nonmaternity silk blouse I decided I had to wear beneath my jumper wouldn't pop its last button. To fit into it I had to leave all but the neck button open; I felt nearly undressed but at least I had a change of outfit.

The very thought of stepping onto the dance floor seemed indecorous. People swirled around me; I felt like a statue coaxed into standing, walking. At one-thirty I told David we had to go home.

Ten more days and counting. My students took their final, I came down with a sore throat. When I felt better, I spoke to friends who called, eager for news. They apologized for bothering me. I was touched by their concern, but knew I sounded remote. "I'll call you as soon . . ."

I woke up on January 10 to find my left thumb twitching,

perhaps a sign of other muscular activity to come. Leah and her mother visited; seeing the girl was like a potion for all that ailed me. I asked her where her father, a novelist, was. "Making bookie," she said. After lunch I took the bus to Dr. Peters, noting how I hoisted myself up and down steps, got in and out of seats, beds, clothing; that I knew the location of every public bathroom on my route to anywhere; that I sleepwalked to the bathroom at home three or four times a night—all compromises to my pregnancy accruing at once.

I weighed in at 168 pounds, two more than my father at the end of his nine-month diet. My cervix was soft but not dilated. "A great sign," Sue told me, but I didn't believe her. At home I scrubbed the kitchen and bathroom, shaved my legs, cleaned my ears, cut my finger- and toenails. Then it was evening; David came home. Then it was the morning of January 11 and I was officially late.

A friend once argued for the creation of "dead of winter," a new season to follow winter proper and precede spring. With the passing of my due date, I found myself there. A cold snap became a spell, snow fell and fell, wind chill factors stole fifty degrees from the temperature. Babies come after snowstorms, I heard from a friend; this baby was going to come after everything, it seemed. He'd already outlasted my fears about the delivery. This was nature's way to cure anxiety, forcing me to shrug and say, What the hell, just let it happen.

The phone began ringing. David and I jolted each time, as if the caller had news for us—news that we had had the baby. From us our friends only learned that there were two shootings in our neighborhood, that the baby ice-skated over the top of my vagina, that we'd call . . .

Throughout my pregnancy, every woman I had asked told me

not only the lovingly embroidered story of her own labor, but also the story of her best friend, or her sister, which contrasted with or reinforced hers. All the details were recounted as if the experience had been fossilized the instant the baby swam out. Each woman's voice took on the timbre of a professional storyteller, with irony, suspense, anticipation at her command, until finally—the happy ending. With such clear rising action, climax, and denouement, the story of birth is artistically shaped even when told in a rush, as it usually was, from women who couldn't at first believe that I was really interested, who savored each narrative moment as if they'd been hoping for years that someone would ask.

My grandmother called nearly every day to give me the same message: "It's not so bad. Labor pains are like menstrual cramps," she told me. "Don't be afraid." Her own mother had delivered her last child, her eighth, by herself rather than disturb the midwife who was dozing at the foot of the bed. And her friend Sadie, the one who had screamed with such wracking intensity, admitted after her child was born that she only had carried on that way because she thought she was supposed to.

The uncle who had asked me to hold off until his birthday, January 18, called to say, "Keep trying." Another friend called because she had a dream that I had delivered. We seemed to be invading the psychic space of everyone we knew. And then we were out of Capricorn and into Aquarius.

I took off my earrings and wedding band. I stared into my closet and tried to imagine ever fitting into my gray suit skirt with its slit up the side.

Maybe I'd simply begin growing smaller, little by little.

The house needed recleaning and my legs reshaving. Friends began a second round of phone calls. Each day I resolved to cook and freeze dinners for future use, but never finished composing my shopping list.

.   .   .

At Dr. Peters's office I met a woman who looked like me. I asked her when she was due. "I had my daughter two weeks ago," she said pertly. Oh God, I thought, this never ends.

"He's putting on the finishing touches," the doctor teased. "He wants to be perfect."

But I wasn't in the mood for jokes. "You'll deliver before the weekend," she said soberly, instructing me once again to phone her when the contractions were ten minutes apart and lasting one minute. She explained that if I called when my water broke in the middle of the night, I'd have a sleepy doctor delivering me in the morning. "Don't panic."

"What if I don't go into labor?" I asked wearily. "Do I see you again next week?"

"Don't worry," she said. "You'll deliver."

"But what if I don't?"

"I'm not wrong about these things." We were standing on opposite sides of her desk, neither of us smiling. I wasn't budging. She picked up her next chart, put on her glasses and said, not looking up, "Call Saturday morning."

"Thank you," I said, turning to go, thinking I had won.

"But you won't," she called after me.

We discover a wooden closet built into the wall behind our bed by the previous tenants, full of toys, dolls, music boxes, puzzles, clowns, an endless cache.

Days and nights blended. I couldn't forget the song from the childbirth movies which accompanied each birth. I didn't want clutter in my head. I wanted my mind blank to soak in every detail afresh, in my own way. Damn those movies.

Randy called. She had to see her doctor in the city; could she sleep over? I said sure without asking David, who was busily trying to meet the deadline for his last paper of the term—Thursday, January 21.

"Randy wants to come tomorrow," I told him. He said that would be fine. "It may be the last night we're alone," I said.

"Look," he said, barely looking up, "we have to live our lives."

On Wednesday night my mother called. I told her that Lanugo was thrashing around mercilessly. "We used to call you Thumper," she said, "because you thumped so much." Then she told me that en route to her Cesarean section, she asked her doctor if he knew how deep he had to cut. What she remembered next was waking up and having her mother reach across the bed to pat her hand and say, "You made the grade."

I smiled. We'd run out of stories. Wasn't there something else to say? We'd speak tomorrow or as soon as there was any news.

We each said goodbye, and then a moment before she hung up, she said, "God be with you."

5

Giving Birth

THE NEXT DAY, Thursday, David and I were in the supermarket that had just reopened after a fire, buying dinner for Randy who would be staying overnight. He had rushed home after delivering the paper I'd typed the previous evening. I'd spent the morning at home, writing in my journal, showering for the first time in days with the newly restored hot water, visiting Nan and Leah, unable to shake a good mood.

I was brandishing a box of linguine on sale when I half heard, half felt a tiny internal pop like a cork loosened on a private bottle of champagne tucked in my pelvis. I stood with my legs together, trying to prevent water from sloshing on the clean supermarket floor.

"David," I said, "my water just broke." We put down the items we were carrying—hamburger, apple juice—and David asked me if I was sure.

We had our first fight, on our honeymoon, during a game of badminton when he questioned my calling his shot out of bounds by asking, "Are you sure?" He likes certainty. "My pants are soaking," I assured him. I made him walk behind me to see if the leak was visible. The four-block walk home loomed long. On the street, progressing slowly like an old couple, we both thought that within twenty-four hours the baby would be born. It was a wet, slushy gray afternoon. I wasn't sure of the date.

Upstairs I headed for the bathroom and sat on the toilet while David called the doctor's office and proclaimed, "Roberta has broken her waters," in a tone that made us all laugh. It was about three in the afternoon.

I had my first contraction in the bathroom. It came from nowhere—an internal tornado picked up and hurled every organ toward my skin but nothing showed outwardly; the force was wholly absorbed. I couldn't recognize my own body in the pain. I endured two before the words came to me: I am in labor. The bald experience was so overwhelming that I couldn't locate the words for what felt like minutes until a simple, comprehensible sentence yoked them.

David urged me to move to the bed. I hesitated; I was still leaking. He insisted. Taking out our little brown spiral notebook which I had bought only two days earlier, small enough to fit in a shirt pocket, he wrote down the time and duration of the contraction. He had a digital watch and used the lap counter, as if he were running.

We expected another contraction in about ten minutes, so David called our parents. I'd promised scads of people that I'd call at the first tremor. They were forgotten.

I interrupted David on the phone. Something was amiss, the next contraction on its way. Assuming that I was in the first stage of labor, I began the appropriate breathing technique—carefully paced inhalations followed by gently blown exhalations. It worked in the sense that without it I'd have been swallowed by the pain and with it I could contend. But I had never been less distracted in my life. Nothing else was in my universe but the pain.

The contraction lasted nearly a full minute. Didn't that mean I was in the second stage of labor? David wasn't sure either. Trying to figure it out, I felt the remote clutches of another gathering contraction. Instead of alerting David so he could begin timing and coaching me, I ignored it. Maybe it wouldn't . . . But it did come, full blown, and I had to breathe too quickly to make up for the time I had cheated on. David, working his watch and keeping notes, asked if we should switch to the next breathing technique. It was three-thirty; I'd been in labor one half hour.

Randy arrived. "Roberta's in labor," David proclaimed. She ran into the bedroom. I was between contractions, actually dozing off out of sheer exhaustion, and I asked, "Would you like something to drink?"

Then I was pulled back, forced to drop out of the conversation, out of the realm of friendly discourse, to retreat into a world unaccompanied, and I saw my husband and friend through the wrong end of a close-up lens—remote, stranded, blessedly pain-ignorant.

This is how it must feel to be mad, I thought. People suffering from delusions can't tell you about their world, can only play out its devastating effects. You have to believe me. "Do you believe me?" I asked David with my eyes.

Months later I had a dream that perfectly captured my experience of labor:

I am in a huge warehouse in a metal contraption resembling a lifeguard's chair, strapped in so that I am leaning forward, caught off balance, defying gravity, suspended. I can't right myself nor fall forward as would be natural. It's semidark. I'm alone and voiceless. Every cell is alive with the longing to fall, to tumble to the ground. But I am pinned.

The contractions came increasingly quickly and lasted a long time. The breathing techniques worked but only to a limited extent. I stared, as I was supposed to, at something on the wall—a print we brought back from Sweden of the crown prince on horseback. I thought of the panorama from the float in the lake in Hinsdale. But only for seconds at a time. My mind wasn't in my mind but in my gut, deep inside, where Lanugo was first made.

Sue, our gynecologist friend, called when she came home from work and offered to come right over. My mother called and I talked until the rumbling began and then I simply dropped the receiver.

David hurriedly called the doctor. "Don't worry," she said. "I won't be at the hospital until seven. You arrive then too." I heard my Lamaze teacher say, "Stay home as long as possible. Babies don't fall out."

But *I* kept falling out of this world and into another. In the absence of contractions I felt more elation than I'd ever known—a chemical, a hormone dripping into my system and making me soar. I asked Randy to massage my foot; I told David not to forget my journal. But then the chemistry switched, my system over-loaded, the elation shattered, turned to something indigestible in my stomach, my veins; I left for my thousand-mile-long journey. David was on his own now.

Breathe, always breathe. I wanted to inhale and not breathe again till I came out the other side.

Sue arrived for her house call breezy and competent. "I brought a pair of sterile gloves," she said, "so I can check your dilation whenever you want. Let's put on the radio. Enjoy it. Let's take a picture."

The print developed before our eyes. I looked like raw pain, like a big dumb lost animal. "No more pictures," I barked. "And turn off that damn radio."

"Talk to me," David said. "Don't shut me out. How are you feeling?" In Lamaze we were told to be sure to communicate. No one ever mentioned not wanting to.

"I really can't talk," I said. I needed to stay closed, shut down, unable to let even breath out. I wanted him there but quietly, not touching me. He wasn't admitted where I was.

Our doorbell rang—the super asked if we could leave the kitchen faucet open all night so the pipes wouldn't freeze again. The sound of running water broke my concentration. I lost the rhythm of the breathing techniques and screamed. David tried to lead me back to the pattern of inhalations but I switched automatically into second gear, the one I wasn't supposed to need until the second stage of labor, hours from now. It was four o'clock.

Sue took charge. She sat next to me, pressed two fingers on the hump of my stomach. "The contraction's starting now," she said, and I wanted to kill her, the messenger with the bad news. "It's peaking, it's going down now," she reported, a split second before I could feel it. She was right every time. I wanted her never to leave me.

"You're doing great," my coaches cheered. I wasn't sure what that meant. I couldn't talk with pain. What exactly was I doing great? Surviving? If I could have thought of an escape, I would have. As the pain mounted, became uncontainable, strangled me, we called the doctor again.

"You won't deliver before eleven or twelve tonight," she said. It was now five-thirty.

Another strangling contraction. "That was a good one," Sue said. How did she mean that? In the way cold showers are good? In the sense that mothers smack their newly menstruating daughters? "I think we should try to get you dressed now."

We had waited too long; I couldn't move. She helped me up, asked for my clothes. She slipped me into a jumper, knee socks, my down jacket. I would never make it down the hall of the apartment, much less to the hospital. David rang for the elevator and I had a contraction before we reached the front door.

Randy offered to run to the store and buy David a sandwich to last him through the night. He ordered a salami on rye and a Doctor Pepper. I concentrated on not having a contraction in the elevator, sparing my neighbors. As soon as we landed, the contraction erupted and I huddled against the radiator. An elderly woman resident, I couldn't turn to see who, tiptoed around me.

"She's not dying," Sue said, "just having a baby." Another contraction met me in the vestibule. David appeared in a cab. For months we had joked about being able to reach the hospital in the middle of the worst blizzard, a mere block away, yet we ended up scaring a cab driver into breaking all the lights as he circled one-way streets to the hospital entrance.

"I have three," he said. "Lots of luck," showing more kindness than the hospital admitting officer. I sustained three hard, out-of-control contractions leaning against a glass wall in the lobby while we debated whether to use my maiden or married name, an issue I thought we had settled weeks before.

As I was led upstairs, I told David that if I was only half dilated and counting on four more hours I'd take anything they offered me. Anything.

Upstairs, David and I were separated ("Don't let them separate you," we'd been told, but we had no voice to argue). "It will only be for a few moments," a kind nurse promised, "till he gowns up and you get prepped." Helping me inside, beyond the swinging doors, she heard me through one choking contraction and said, "You're in transition, honey"—labor's last stage before delivery. "Try to give me some urine and take off your clothes." She showed me into a tiny bathroom in which I could do neither.

By six-thirty I was on the examination table and the nurse bet the skeptical resident that I was fully dilated. He bemusedly examined me. "Ten centimeters," he said in disbelief. I felt like crying. David came rushing in wearing a green gown and a mask.

"I'm there," I said. I should have begun pushing hours ago; no wonder the pain was so bad. Every part of my body wanted to push but the nurse and resident told me not to, if I wanted my own doctor to deliver me. They had already phoned her office and she was on her way.

Meanwhile David abandoned words and told me to do what he did. He drew a deep breath in, then out. I stared at the enormous clock dead center on the wall in front of me, a comforting sight. Its elongated hands and huge numbers mark time. Time passed. The nurse went to call the doctor again. "It's coming," I scream, "the head, I can feel it."

That's it, we can't wait any more: someone makes a decision. I am moved onto a stretcher and wheeled down the hall into the delivery room—no prep, no I.V., no birthing room, no mirrors in position so I can see what's coming. Still no private obstetrician. The resident hastily introduces himself and begins numbing me for the episiotomy. "Don't push, don't push," they warn; I can hardly avoid it. Finally I get the go-ahead. "Push, push," they chorus. I scream with something close to ecstasy. Then my doctor bustles in holding a mask to her face.

"Rotate the head, rotate," she says, assuming her place. "I never heard anything like this for a first labor."

"Push?" I ask. She nods, and I do and something passes. The head is out. "What is it?" I ask my husband. "What is it?" He is standing to my right, seeing what I cannot.

"It's a boy or a girl," he says. "All I can see is the head."

"Wait, don't push," they tell me. Finally the green light. One more push, one more abandoned scream for every part of my straining body and he comes out, entirely out, a boy; I hear my husband admire his testicles. It is 6:56: the nurse notes the time. I see him held up, one hand on his bottom and one on his neck. His profile is imprinted first; black hair, a sleek Mohican look. A sloped forehead, like a Pharaoh.

Then, almost more remarkable than the baby himself comes a thick, heavy roped, translucent umbilical cord, looking as if it were made out of futuristic plastic. It is severed before my eyes.

The pains stop instantly. No more contractions. My mind forms its first sentence. The baby is taken and David and I are in wonderment. "A son," I say to him, "a boy." I had so expected a girl. David tells me to look down, that my stomach must be flat. It is. A boy. What will I do with a boy? The doctor works out the placenta, which I don't even notice, and begins to sew. The mood is jolly, everyone incredulous over the quickness of my labor. David takes some instant pictures, one of us looking at a picture taken the moment before. The doctor admires her stitchery. The baby is being tended but we all think how lovely that he hears laughter, sounds of life and love.

Finally he is handed to me, a swaddled stalk. His face is wrinkled and doughy, his hair slicked back. "Benjamin?" I ask his father. As I am wheeled into the recovery room, Benjamin is placed by my side and he sucks, just as he is supposed to.

I am required to spend an hour in recovery even though I feel fine, perfect. David leaves to make his calls, the baby is whisked to the nursery to be weighed, the nurses clean me, take vital signs, the doctor fills out forms. The minutes drag. I am fine, better than fine; can't I leave? In ten minutes . . .

As I am wheeled to my room, I glimpse Sue and my parents gathered at the nursery window across the wall. I call and everyone comes running, my father first. "You have a grandson," I say. He stoops to kiss me and says, "Thank you."

We gather in the room; my bed is closest to the window. David's parents arrive to fill up every inch. Everyone hears the story of my remarkable labor twice before leaving at ten. David stays. We hear a rumbling in the hall, the sound of babies in their plastic cribs leaving the nursery to find their mothers. Benjamin's crib says: "Boy Weiser—No Formula." His hair is clean and combed; he's asleep. We don't unwrap him, count fingers or toes. We simply watch him. Then they leave, father and son, to return at 10:00 A.M. and 2:00 A.M. respectively. I am alone.

I don't sleep for one second. Twice that night a nurse comes in to awaken me before handing me Ben, who sucks desultorily, but I am already completely awake, every cell in my brain straining for awareness. I review the day in detail, its every shadow and color. I have no sense of the baby except that he is out of me. The invader has left. He comes to visit, a tidy bundle; he doesn't cry, his eyes are wide and eager to please like a polite guest.

I feel proud, wish I could curl up and hug myself for coming through so well, so alertly. I take most of the credit, but silently thank my Lamaze teacher. Her method worked! Not perfectly, not according to the plan I'd studied, but well enough to enable me to give the performance of my life. And then I think of David. I try to hold in my mind the scope of the new commitment into which we have entered, and I suddenly miss him with a new fervor, want him close by me now, touching me as much as I didn't want his touch before. But he is at home, in our bed, making phone calls to the sound of running water, not sleeping either, I am sure.

"Are you sure he's ours?" David asks again and again the next day, even though he witnessed the solemn ceremony affixing ID bracelets to mother and son moments after birth. I assure David that I'd know Ben's profile anywhere. He's ours.

My grandmother calls the next morning, among others, but it isn't until a conversation with her a few weeks later, when I am home, that I remember what I want to tell her. "Listen," I begin. "It hurt like hell. A hundred times worse than the worst menstrual cramps."

"Of course, darling," she says. "Aren't you glad I didn't tell you the truth?"

6

The First Three Months
Bonding

*F*OR THREE DAYS I rested in the hospital while my spirit took off for a strange place, a place defined by its not being where anyone else was. I wasn't exactly on vacation—I was bleeding through my hospital gown, my episiotomy stitches killed me, my uterus contracted painfully with each of Ben's hearty sucks. Yet I was far enough away from the ice storms I glimpsed outside my window to be surprised when all my visitors showed up cold and wet. We seemed to inhabit different weather.

Twice a day the room swelled with friends and family bearing baby presents and huge, redolent bouquets of flowers which spilled over into my roommate's side of the room. Several times a day the baby carts rumbled through the hallways. I learned to tell time by these comings and goings.

David came early each morning, the hospital both close and small enough to seem like an extension of our apartment. He brought the newspapers and a vase for which he never bought flowers. In these ways he attempted to reclaim my anonymous hospital room. But even as we shared phone calls with far-away friends, even as we admired our son together, held him, cooed to him, David's eyes asked me, "Where in the world *are* we?" And I telegraphed back: "Wish you were here."

My roommate was bedridden after her C-section. Her husband visited only at night, and she spent the long hours waiting for him, blowing into a plastic contraption designed to relieve gas pains. "Gas is worse than stitches," she told me, smiling weakly, as I bounded from bed to bathroom to sitz baths to the scale David had searched out. ("Now don't be upset," said the nurse, helping me out of robe and slippers. 155. Only 35 pounds more to lose.) My roommate looked lovely in a delicate pink nightgown, the way women who had just given birth look in the movies and on television. I felt like apologizing for my activity.

And Benjamin? He appeared in the room and stayed until he was taken away. From the first he was a student, intent on lifting his head, shifting his gaze, pondering his environment. Although he ate and yawned with gusto, I held him as if he were breakable, awed by his integrity even in his tininess, afraid to unwrap him, to move suddenly around him. The nurses found this more than comical. With manners bordering on the gruff, they stroked his head with the hard, flat part of their hands, swung him from shoulder to football hold, and swaddled him in flannel blankets in one deft motion as crisply as a baker easing a sliced rye into a waxed bag.

To these intimidating caretakers I had to reveal the scope of my ignorance—that I didn't know the first thing about holding, burping, feeding, changing, diapering, dressing, or bathing my son. My ineptitude embarrassed me and astounded them. "Oh come on now, Mrs. Weiser," one nurse said. "You can't be *serious.*" I'd asked her whether the tapes on disposable diapers go in the back or front. I wasn't born knowing how to type, either, I felt like telling her. Why should I inherently know how to diaper? But I kept my mouth shut. As angry as I was at the nurses, I needed them—one of them—to tell me what to do before I went home.

For a while on Sunday it seemed as if our departure would be delayed. Ben's pediatrician, Dr. Thomas Sands, remarked during his routine morning visit that Ben had developed jaundice. "It's nothing to be concerned about," he said, and I let him assure me. He was the only pediatrician David and I had interviewed, proving ourselves no better at doctor shopping than we had been when we had had to choose an obstetrician. But Tom was young, had a gentle manner, and came with Nan's highest praise. In fact, we had heard her talk about him so much that we quite naturally began calling him Tom, too. He didn't seem to mind.

Tom said it would take about an hour for the latest blood test results to come back which would determine Ben's discharge. I could opt to stay if he stayed, or go home to get some rest. So many times I'd heard Nan aver that she trusted Tom with her daughter's life. I trusted Nan. And now I had to trust him.

At first the prospect of staying another night dismayed me. But if problems could develop so unexpectedly in the hospital, the air outside seemed suddenly fraught with unknown dangers. I decided I'd welcome staying. But on the heels of this realization came the word: we were both released.

Did that mean we could simply leave? Removing Ben's hospital garments was terrifying. Now the clothes I supplied would have to keep him warm. My mother helped me dress him in five layers of the tiniest sizes we had, all too big. Then she packed up the flowers and packets of free samples and coupons from the hospital, and shepherded me down to the lobby. A nurse gave David the baby to hold while I gingerly negotiated the ice at the curb. I held the baby on my lap as David drove us, in absolutely blinding sunshine, the half block home.

Our homecoming had all the trappings of the real thing but it didn't last. Within twenty-four hours Ben would be back in the hospital, an emergency admission. But on Sunday our house was abuzz with happy activity. My father assembled Ben's crib; Marian, who had come up from Washington to stay as long as we needed her, was cooking dinners for the next week; my mother tracked down vases in which to place the flowers. We all ate lunch together—Ben too; he woke up crying, for the first time. Friends came by and left, the Super Bowl game, which David had left on without the sound, was over, and by five o'clock my parents had gone too. I was glad to get down to family life at home, but relieved that Marian wasn't leaving. She had recently stayed with a family after the birth of their daughter; she had experience. David and I were too fragile a unit to be left completely alone.

All day I had rebuffed advice to take it easy. "I feel fine," I'd protested, unable to gauge what I had been through. But Sunday night I began to feel the toll. When Ben cried, there was no nurse to hand me a cleanly wrapped infant to feed. I had to get up, turn on the light, pick him up. Soggy. Should I change him first while he's bawling, or feed him right away? Why hadn't I asked a nurse? Because I hadn't known enough to pose the question until now. How many things was it possible not to know? I don't remember how many times Ben awoke, how the night passed, or how I allowed David to leave in the morning to attend a class. By eleven o'clock Monday morning I felt as if I'd aged twenty years, and the mere prospect of having something else to do, even if it was bundling up the baby and walking him over to the hospital to have his blood tested, seemed as welcome as any I'd ever entertained.

Ben's bilirubin count was high, much higher than the day before.

The resident was dour. "He should never have been released," she told me, leading me to an office where I was to call my pediatrician, Tom, to report Ben's count. Tom wanted a blood retest at four in the afternoon, and recommended that it take place at the downtown hospital where he was on staff in case Ben had to be admitted. But the decision to change hospitals was up to me.

So this was motherhood. Making decisions about hospitalizations in a cubbyhole of an office with my baby squirming and turning yellow. It was more comforting to think of Ben in this hospital, close by, but in the end I chose to heed the doctor's suggestion.

For the next four hours I tried to interest Ben in breast feeding. He wanted nothing to do with it. The pediatrician explained that this was typical of jaundiced babies. "It may be best to stop for a while," he said, breast milk being too efficiently digested to wash the bilirubin out of his system.

This was a situation I was prepared for: the male doctor who secretly hates nursing despite lip service to the contrary, and shows his true colors at the first opportunity. Be staunch in these cases, the books had advised. Don't be dissuaded.

"If you have strong feelings about nursing," Tom went on, "I'll support you. But it's your decision."

He kept saying that. Decision-making was never my strength. But David wasn't home, Benjamin was wailing—I had to act. I asked what type of formula to use and sent Marian to the drugstore.

By three, David was home; we rebundled Ben, hailed a cab, stopped at a local baby store to pick up a manual breast pump for me, as per another direction from the doctor, and headed downtown through rush hour traffic with Ben on my lap.

It was already dark and turning sharply colder when we reached the lab a few moments before closing time. We waited nearly an hour, long enough to attempt an aborted feeding and then a bungled diaper changing on a chair. Ben cried inconsolably, ceaselessly. The technician who finally called his name was non-plussed to see a days-old infant, and made me hold him supine on a couch while she tried to coax blood from his heel into her glass vial. It took ten minutes. This is a situation during which people faint, I told myself. David left the room. The nurse began sweating visibly. Ben's crying reached a new intensity.

Waiting for the results, trying to feed Ben, with Marian and David hovering close and everyone else gone, I realized I could no longer feel my spine. I hadn't brought any more diapers or another bottle. I realized that if Ben didn't come home with us I could have a night's sleep.

What kind of monster would wish her newborn in the hospital? Endless self-recriminations would have followed had not we then received Ben's bilirubin count—a dangerously high 18. We phoned Tom, who issued his most terrifying instruction in a day full of instructions: Admit him emergency. "It's most likely a lab error," he said, but he was taking no chances. It finally dawned on me that Ben was sick as we rushed him in a frozen wind across a courtyard to the main wing of the hospital.

"Who's the mother here?" asked a young doctor straddling a chair across from me. After handing Ben over to a nurse on the pediatrics floor, I'd collapsed into a rocking chair feeling as old and heavy as my grandmother.

He explained that Ben was having another more accurate blood test and soon I'd have one too. Ben's bilirubin level indicated that something besides normal neonatal jaundice was going on. He was concerned about a possible blood incompatibility. That might necessitate a complete blood transfusion—a tricky but not necessarily critical procedure. Too much bilirubin accumulating in Ben's tissues could lead to brain damage. Did I have any questions.

Brain damage?

"Unlikely," the doctor said. He indicated a waiting room down the hall where we could rest or stay overnight if we wished.

Sleep here? My only relief was in knowing I could leave. For the first time I noticed where I was—a huge room with several metal cribs. In one was a six-year-old girl with a swollen head, in another a young Korean girl, both attended by their mothers, young women who moved about the room as efficiently and mindlessly as if they were in their own kitchens.

I needed to pump my breasts, tend to my stitches, find a pay phone. My mother was near tears. "Bring Ben to us," she said, to her house, to the general practitioner who had treated me as a child, and to the local hospital.

I told her we were in the best hospital in the city. My father wanted to drive in. I said no. I could hardly talk. Marian said we should get a bite to eat.

When we returned, we found Ben lying naked on a diaper in a plastic isolette near the window. A nurse was placing a blindfold over his eyes and a patch over his genitals. He was screaming. His little heel was bloody. "We're not sure of the long-term effects of phototherapy," the nurse said, turning on a long fluorescent bulb like the one on my desk.

As if on cue, the room seemed to empty, to quiet down. For a moment David and I were alone. "Is he going to die?" I asked David, abandoning myself for the first time that day to hysteria.

He shook his head no, clutched my hand. Minutes passed. Tom appeared in the doorway; he wouldn't have come if this weren't serious. How many more signs did we need? "Still waiting," he said.

"My wife just asked me if Ben is going to die," David said, crying.

"He won't die," the doctor said. He searched out our eyes and locked firmly into our gaze. "You shouldn't say that," I felt like telling him, "you have no guarantee." But I believed him, and thanked him.

It was nearly nine o'clock. The other children in the room went to sleep, their mothers rocking in chairs near the cribs. Then Tom appeared in the doorway, face as bright as New Year's Eve. "Sixteen," he said jubilantly: 16, the first test was a lab error after all. The technician had probably broken blood cells in the sample she was trying to draw. Ben's count was still high enough to keep him in the hospital but low enough to rule out everything save normal neonatal jaundice—no blood incompatibilities, transfusions, damage. We were paralyzed with relief.

Another decision had to be made. If I stayed overnight, as the other mothers did, now gathering their things, saying goodnight, I could give Ben his bottle every four hours, hold him, change him. If I went home, I could take a bath, soak my sore bottom, sleep: sleep. I desperately wanted to leave but hated how thoroughly I wanted this, and let the others, David and Marian, talk me into the reasonableness of going home, taking care of myself. We'd come back tomorrow, we could phone the hospital every four hours to hear the new count. Ben had grown quiet in his crib, whimpering, stirring. David took my hand, the nurse turned off the overhead light; the only light in the room came from Ben's cage.

Several months later, Marian helped me realize that not wanting Ben to come home that night wasn't the same as wishing him sick in the hospital. At first I couldn't see this, but separating the two feelings, as if by distillation, made sense. I wasn't a gorgon, simply an exhausted new mother. My labor may have been short but it was still intense. These first days of motherhood should have found me in bed, the baby handed to me for feedings and caressing. Waking up to phone the hospital for bilirubin counts, rush through breakfast, and jump in a taxi downtown was not the usual way to be initiated into parenthood.

But I couldn't shake the notion that while mine may have been a crash course, we all had the same curriculum to master, sooner or later.

Ben looked like a chicken in an oven. His genital patch was off, his feces baking on his skin. I summoned a nurse who looked unperturbed by her lapse, changed and cleaned him while informing me that phototherapy was discovered by a nun in a convent hospital who noticed babies placed near windows didn't turn yellow.

Then she handed me my son, swaddled in a blanket, and his bottle. I fed him; he didn't seem to notice. When I returned him to his crib, I sought out the doctor who had admitted us. From the midst of today's emergency he said to me, "The count plateaus before it drops. Maybe thirty-six more hours." Clearly we were yesterday's crisis.

The next two days assumed a comforting sameness. At one point Marian left and my sister Annie arrived in her stead, but I still spent mornings at home, and afternoons in the hospital. The other mothers in the room kept track of Ben for me when I wasn't there, reporting one day that he had nearly crawled out of his crib during the night, nosing his way to the edge with resolve unbeliev-able in a newborn. "He really wants out of there," they told me. In my sunny corner of the room I suctioned my breasts with a manual breast pump and proudly studied my determined young son. It finally seemed time to take him home.

On Thursday morning the hospital advised me to bring clothes for Ben; his count had indeed plummeted, and we could leave. By the time Annie and I arrived we found Ben on David's lap, already discharged. The light in his crib was dark, the case cover opened, his discarded masks lying inside like party rubbish. All eyes were on us as I dressed him, making me fumble all the more.

"Goodbye," everyone in the room chorused, genuinely happy to see us leave. "Good luck." I found myself unable to respond in kind. I hope I forget all of you and this entire room, all these days immediately and forever, I thought to myself. I knew I never would.

On the way to the elevator we passed the admitting doctor. "What's the matter?" he asked. "You look sad around the mouth."

"Nothing," I said. "We're going home." Damn you, I thought; damn you and your sharp eyes.

"Well," he replied. "Good luck." David had already hailed a

taxi and Annie ushered us out. Then we sped uptown and for the second, less auspicious but final time, we brought Benjamin home. He was eight days old.

My memories of the first weeks at home are very selective. I remember the frantic call I put through to Tom on the Thursday we returned. Ben had been at my breasts continuously, for about an hour, and cried when I attempted to stop feeding him. Would this go on forever?

"Give him ten minutes on a side, that's all," Tom said. "And wait at least two hours between feedings. At this rate he'll eat your nipples raw." He already had.

Armed with medical sanction, I deposited Ben on his aunt's lap—Annie didn't seem to find his cries as unbearable as I did. She propped her nephew on her lap and picked up the *National Geographic* she had been reading.

In my bath, to which I'd retreated in nervous tears, I heard her reading, in her gentlest tone, about the mating habits of kangaroos. Ben was quiet. My own reading material was a newly released book about the effects of nuclear war. I read it quite beyond my will, aware that the future the author was describing now had Ben's face on it. "He's asleep," Annie called in. "Should I put him in his crib?"

"I guess so." But when I came out of the bath, I found him comfortably nestled on her lap.

On the weekend Annie went home our house was full of grandparents. I stayed in a nightgown. Not the pretty new ones I'd purchased but a hand-me-down from my grandmother. Food stockpiled in the refrigerator turned bad; flowers rotted in their vases; packages accumulated in the spare room. What went on in the rest of the house went on without my control. I made only guest appearances in the other rooms, shuttling incessantly between bed and bathroom.

"He's so cute, so precious," his grandparents chanted. And he was: his tiny fingernails, mother-of-pearl tears, curled fists, heart-shaped lower lip. His perfect tininess was breathtaking and impossible, but it also hinted of terror. He was so brave, so valiant, every muscle in him straining toward awareness, some elementary kind of mastery. His vulnerability brought me to tears; his rawness, his entirety overwhelmed me, pierced through my consciousness as nothing else ever had. To call him "cute" angered me; such blatant sentimentality on the part of my family infuriated me. What a shallow response to this new person, my son. He deserved something more original, profound, genuine. He was all too real.

Yet I acknowledged this best alone. Some kind of petulance kept me from feeling effusive in the presence of visitors. Perhaps the real root of this was simple jealousy at the way Ben could contentedly fall asleep in another's arms. I wanted every moment of my son to myself, convinced that no one else felt for him what I did. Yet a moment later, as his neediness began to devour me, I'd feel compelled to remind those around me that he was less a complex organism than a single-celled creature, a long tract from mouth to anus for whose maintenance I was responsible.

Every two hours he demanded milk from my body. But first came a diaper change. Twelve times a day I had to pore over his genitals, his bottom, with more concentration than I had ever applied to any book. Usually I had to change his undershirt, gown, and crib sheet as well. Next came twenty minutes on the couch, Ben sampling the nipple as if it were a fine cigar before chomping down with such vigor that I winced, me drinking the required glass after glass of water and trying to calculate when to move him to the other breast so that he'd drink his fill and adequately drain my supply. Then came burping, rocking, and coaxing back to sleep. If I were exceptionally lucky, I'd have time to rub vitamin E cream on my nipples and eat a piece of toast before Ben stirred to begin the next cycle.

But sometimes he cried after a feeding, cried for no reason I could discern. Sometimes he woke up only an hour after a previous feeding—then what? "You'll know what his cries mean," I'd been promised. But I didn't. And others who presumed to know angered me. I knew him best, and he was impenetrable to me. Instead of the mystic communion between us that I'd counted on, I relied on a plodding trial-and-error method of running through his needs until hitting on the right one. So much for rapport.

That I responded to him as quickly and thoroughly as I did, that his call roused me as urgently as it did, was surely a form of love. It simply wasn't a type of love with which I was acquainted. This was love on a cellular, biological level. Intimacy, I began to understand, is rooted in the corporal. It has to do with the distance between bodies. None separated mine from my son's. We had both been swallowed by the cave I used to fashion for myself under the covers, that safe, familiar space which traps the odors of your own body—milk, blood, tears, sweat all mingling. This wasn't the romantic intimacy between adults, but an earthbound, often tedious kind which is undertaken, no questions asked.

I wanted to tend to him utterly, and wanted to do nothing at all. I was indignant and enraged when my family couldn't appreciate him as fully as I could, and knew that I didn't want them to. I wanted to be Ben's mother and wanted to be Ben, with someone to mother me.

Was this postpartum blues? I had trouble linking the phrase to my experience, the former sounding so offhanded, something to wait out like a cold or a spell of bad weather. Whereas I felt plunged into something thick, something unexpectedly freezing.

For our first pediatrician visit on Monday morning, I put on a skirt and makeup. But Tom took one look at my face and said, "The first week is a bitch, isn't it?" Why couldn't I hide it? We talked. I had forgotten to bring extra diapers—no, I hadn't yet realized that you never go out of the house without extras. No one told me that diapers without gathers leak. Ben seeped through his onto my knee. I had no change of clothes for him, nothing with which to wipe off my skirt. How was anyone this ignorant allowed out of the house?

"Do you have any questions?" Tom asked.

Did I ever. My problem was getting medical people to acknowledge the level of concrete detail I needed. For example, when I bathed Ben, what should I do with my hands? I mean, where should I put them? How would he get from tub to towel? How warm should the water be?

Tom answered seriously and comprehensively, but quickly. In his waiting room sat at least four other women who all looked enthralled with their babies. I doubted if their questions would sound like this.

"Trust yourself," Tom advised me. He was appealing to the part of me that had an advanced degree, that was a professional. I withered before all the judgment calls I had to make. Suddenly I longed to be home in my nightgown, in the humidified, stuffy bedroom tinted rose by the red calico curtains, in which the outside world—weather, time, instructions—left only faint impressions and shadows. Thankfully, I'd be back here in a week and Tom could correct any serious mistakes I'd made. I wondered if I'd keep coming every week for a year.

Tom laughed. "After next week you come again in two weeks, and then a month later." Oh God, I thought, how will I manage? How will I know if Ben is eating enough? Without my weekly visits, I'll have nothing to do on Mondays, no way to structure the week. Coming here took up hours—simply getting out of my front door took sixty minutes.

"It won't always," Tom said, smiling kindly, rising behind his desk to say goodbye.

. . .

Friends visited during the week, although not as frequently as they would have if I had been able to explain how desperate I was for company. Only Gail came close to realizing this. She arrived one evening at the peak of Ben's crankiness, on the day when David had his latest class. She brought Chinese food for us to share. As I tried to soothe Ben, she followed us and said, "Listen to him! He's so powerful, so full of himself. He has so much to *say.*" She was right. I'd never thought of it quite that way.

On Sunday we had Ben's *b'rith*—ritual circumcision—at our house. More than fifty people came but only a few stood with us as the procedure was performed, Ben's only comfort a gauze pad soaked in a bit of cherry wine. He learned to cry with a new intensity that afternoon, and it took four people three hours to get him to sleep. "Babies don't feel pain," most people told me, looking into my ashen face. I hated them. But I found, as the afternoon wore on, that I didn't want anyone to leave. Soon it would be Sunday night and as exhausted as I was, I didn't want to go to sleep, for once I did it would be Monday morning and then I'd be alone.

"I can't face being alone with him," I cried to David. "I feel frantic, I panic . . . "

"It's all part of the odyssey," he assured me. "We're in it together." But in the morning he gathered his books and left for the day. Everyone always eventually left me alone with my son.

I felt, as I remembered Nan telling me, as if I were in a sleep-deprivation experiment, but that wasn't the whole story. Being wrenched from sleep twice a night was bad enough—the cycle of changing, feeding, burping, and resettling an infant to sleep took only slightly less time by night than by day—but what I really suffered from was the lack of a real bedtime to give meaning to time. Most parents sounded like amnesiacs when describing this early period, and no wonder. Unhinged from time, there is no framework in which to remember. My life felt imploded, deconstructed, disassembled.

I had to preserve the notion that night was different from day, so I took a bath at about nine o'clock, read in bed for about five minutes, nursed Ben, and then informed David that the baby was his to walk, sing to, take into the next room, and rock or otherwise divert until either Ben fell asleep or he could have another feeding —whichever came first.

Desperate, David composed an impromptu lullaby. Marching briskly with the baby in his arms, in the coarsest tone he could muster, he sang:

> In the morning we don't care
> We scratch their eyes, we tear their hair
> But at night, we never fight
> We sleep, sleep, sleep.

The chorus alternated the word "sleep" with a snore, and this was followed by other verses, equally violent and preposterous. The first time Ben heard this song, he was stunned into silence and then instant sleep.

But the song's novelty wore off. One night I had to take a turn in the rocking chair, David too exhausted at one-thirty in the morning to sit up. I began singing "Mockingbird"; I tried reading to him, as my sister had, from a magazine, but he wailed until he got the hiccoughs. He wouldn't stop. "I'll throttle you," I thought, though all I did was pick him up and hold him away from me and give him a shake, to scare him out of his hiccoughs. But in the instant that I pulled him away from my body I was flooded with more intense shame and remorse than I had ever known. "Take him," I cried melodramatically, waking David. "I don't trust myself with him." His cries crawled into my ears like snakes reminding me of my sister's cries when she was an infant. That connection made sense. I wasn't only angry at Ben but also at an earlier scenario, when my baby sister had shown up out of nowhere, crying and crying.

"Roberta." David was nudging me. "The baby's crying."

"No," I said, not opening my eyes. "Ben's right here, nursing." I must have fallen asleep. "It's time for the other breast."

"He needs nursing." For some peculiar reason David was peering into the crib, holding a diaper.

I cradled Ben in my arms. "He's here."

"He's here, in the crib. Look."

I opened my eyes. Benjamin was in the crib, bawling. It was four o'clock, the previous nursing was finished, he needed another, needed to be changed, fed again. I could have sworn . . .

One Saturday afternoon, when Ben was about a month old, my parents, grandmother, aunt, and cousin came to visit. By five o'-clock, Ben was beginning his slow but inexorable journey toward the mild crankiness that would last the evening. No one could comfort him, so I nursed him yet again and retreated to the bedroom. David found me in tears. "Everyone loves the baby more than I do," I told him. He understood perfectly. We were the only ones we could trust not to judge each other.

"Do you think you could ask my mother to come in?" I said. I had an idea. Maybe she could take him for a few hours. What I meant was for a week. A month, maybe a year. I needed time to sleep, to catch my breath, to reassess.

I heard muffled whispering inside. Then my mother came in.

Ben had drifted off to sleep. She sat on the bed next to me, held my hand.

I didn't know where to begin. "Was it hard, for you?" I asked. What a question. I needed her to say, "Yes, it was as difficult and impossible as you are finding it, I would have told you if I could." But then she'd be talking about me, *me.*

"It *is* hard," she said gently. "Remember, we lived with my mother until you were two and a half." She had a look I'd never seen before, one that said, "Forgive me if I didn't prepare you better." And I knew that she'd never take Ben. How could I have even considered asking? She'd done her time on the front lines; all she wanted now was her grandmaternal privilege.

"Take a nap," she suggested. "You need your rest. Sleep when he sleeps." I nodded, numb. She paused near the crib on her way out. In the living room the others were setting the table. If Ben cooperated, I could at least eat a normal meal before he woke.

"You know," she began, "your grandmother used to hold you at the window for hours so I could sleep, get the housework done. She always said you had to be *rubig* around a baby." That meant quiet, peaceful, but it also implied a steadiness, a quietude at the core of one's soul.

I too had held Ben at the window. Sometimes I had visualized him falling out of my arms, through the glass, a horrible accident. Ghastly. The grieving mother. A book I had read mentioned the fact that it wasn't unusual for a new mother to think of her newborn having an accident. A foot caught in a flame. An accidental drowning. Don't worry, the book assured me. Many women do. It will pass.

But that didn't begin to explore the true horror of what was happening inside my head. My own baby? What kind of monster thinks about her baby having an accident? That I did think this—not once but frequently—was the most astonishing piece of news I'd ever telegraphed to myself.

Yet at other times I stood at the window with Ben and sang him songs and thought about my grandmother who was born in Russia, who sang to me, who taught me to play scales on a toy piano. I would think: A negligent mother wouldn't do this, stand at the window and show her son the world, overwhelmed by how bound up their lives were, how well they fit together.

I still didn't feel swept away by love; my life was still too disrupted, fragmented, and new. But I was beginning to sense that the only way for me to become the kind of love-struck mother I'd always expected to be was to allow myself the surprising mixture of feelings in which I was now immersed—to acknowledge, accept even the moments of horrifying fantasy. It was a path I'd have to negotiate all by myself. But women with far fewer resources than I had had succeeded as mothers. And I knew that I could no longer define myself without Benjamin at my side.

My mother adjusted Ben's covers on her way out. "He's beautiful," she said, only part statement. It was part plea; I think, even though I'd said nothing, that I scared her. She was asking me if I couldn't mute some of my uncompromising honesty, if I couldn't hurry up and find in my son what she'd already found.

At my three-week checkup, Dr. Peters told me how nicely I was healing and what a perfect body I had for childbearing. "You should have five or six," she said.

"You have five or six," I said, leaving her office in a huff. On the way home I ran into a woman from my Lamaze class rocking a baby carriage. We hugged, though we hadn't been friendly in class. "I have a boy," she said, and there he was, blond and asleep on a sea of pillows, three weeks older than Ben. Her hair was curled and she was wearing makeup and a dress; I was in David's stained down jacket and maternity pants, unable to recall the last time I had seriously looked in a mirror. She shrugged when I asked her how her labor went and didn't ask about mine. Then I complained about having to get up at night.

"Oh, I don't mind getting up for him any more," she said. "We read in Spock that you can let them cry themselves to sleep, and now he only gets up twice a night and I just don't mind."

"Sleep problems, going to bed in infancy, pages 226–28." Without taking off my jacket I consulted the index of Dr. Spock's book, one I had set aside in favor of more modern approaches, all of which stressed comforting the baby no matter what, no matter when. Nothing I had read had breathed a word about letting babies cry. But the item in Spock advised that babies can become over-stimulated and wakeful if parents don't sometimes leave them alone. Crying for fifteen or twenty minutes was okay. In fact, crying was their only emotional outlet. I shoved the book in front of David's nose when he came home for dinner. "We're on, to-night," he said.

After Ben's eleven o'clock feeding, we placed him in his crib on his stomach and turned out the light. He cried. The humidifier was on, a hugely noisy machine, and David and I focused on its roar as we lay on our backs like soldiers, each near our side of the bed, not touching. The digital clock was nearest to me; we had agreed to give Ben ten minutes. My arms hurt from being held so stiffly at my side.

"I don't think I can stand this any more," I said.

"Shut up," David barked, as curtly as I'd ever heard him.

After precisely eight minutes Ben stopped crying. Simply stopped. And fell asleep. "What a perfect baby," I whispered. David didn't reply. The bed was drenched with sweat. Later he got up and kicked the humidifier to shut it off.

.   .   .

The next step, David insisted, was getting a babysitter. David thought I needed time away, and he didn't mean those circular excursions I always seemed to be taking to one doctor or another, punctuated only by undressing and dressing. If I dreaded leaving the house for these, I dreaded coming home more—the wet heat and drawn shades turning the apartment into a kind of swamp I had to wade through, a palpable, tangible barrier separating the world of traffic and conversation from what was inside. My only satisfaction was catching David's expression when I first walked in the door. After only an hour or two, a fraction of my daily portion with the baby, he looked demolished, nearly crazy. "It's unbelievable," I'd prompt him, "being here with Ben."

But he didn't want to talk about what it was like, and certainly didn't want to find out more. He wanted me to get out, like him. When I mentioned that I had no idea how to go about obtaining a competent babysitter, he suggested I call the social service department of the hospital, and they had in their files the name of an agency which specialized in the hourly care of newborns.

Without thinking what I was doing, or what anyone else would think, I entrusted Ben—scarcely three weeks old—to the care of a middle-aged Indonesian woman named Toni, a complete stranger whom I hadn't even interviewed. She washed her hands and changed her shoes before slipping into a white jacket and taking Ben from me. As soon as he was in her arms, I had a complete change of heart: he looked irresistibly cute from the distance of a few inches, quietly cooing as she spoke to him in a language that had no tongue.

David hurried me into the elevator before I could change my mind. He had a big day planned for us. First, a midtown beauty salon, a fashionable place where I couldn't have felt more out of place. To both the girl who washed my hair and the stylist I said, "I have a three-week-old son at home," by way of explanation.

"You should have gotten a Labrador," the haircutter said. "They're easier to train. And they sleep through the night."

My haircut raised my spirits, but David wasn't finished with me. After calling home to make sure Ben was all right—never mind that I wasn't even sure if Toni understood my question—we walked to a deserted Fifth Avenue department store. Spring clothes draped on sneering mannequins seemed just beyond my reach, as if I weren't allowed even to touch them. The thought of a piece of cloth blousing on me, falling gently over my torso, made me dizzy—I was so used to thinking of clothing as the casing and myself as the sausage. Seeing David's eyes feast on the tailored blouses, tucked dresses reminded me of sex, not in its narrow but the broad interpretation: caring about looking pretty, attractive. The return to all this was a train I thought I'd be dying to meet, except that now I simply couldn't remember why. In fact, the entire enterprise seemed ludicrous and moved me to anger. It would require work, another supreme effort, and I felt I had already given more than I ever knew I had. Glimpsing myself in three-way mirrors was triple torture. How could I bear to retain my shapelessness for one more minute; from what dark corner could I scrape up the energy to change? Leave me alone.

David, sensing my depression, picked out a winter coat for me to try on, kimono-style so that my extra bulk didn't impede its lines. It was the only purchase I could have made, yet it was exciting. I had something new and also something to look forward to, moving the belt over a notch as my waistline shrank.

With the coat box under my arm I returned home alone; David went downtown to a class. Ben and Toni had managed very nicely. Ben had slept and hadn't taken the milk, only water, which he'd never taken from me. How had she done it? Could I watch? But with me around Toni grew shy. What did she think of my frivolous new haircut? Why did I care? She left quickly. Back in my arms once more, Ben returned to his fidgety self, and the afternoon quickly turned into the usual early evening blues. Feeling resourceful, I tried on the Snugli, and that worked for a few minutes. David, home for dinner, was moved by the sight of my glamorous hair and Ben on my chest to snap some instant pictures. Why, in every shot, did I look so much like a normal, if unusually tired, person? Was there no shutter speed, no slant of light which would reveal me as I felt: turned inside out?

Toni began coming regularly, and each time I retreated to the spare room, picking my way through the welter of boxes waiting to be organized to my desk where I was supposed to be writing an article. Sleep was all that appealed to me. Sleep when the baby sleeps, everyone always told me, in a tempting, rockabye voice. But how could I sleep away the only moments I was free to be myself—that is, connected with the person I used to be? If I couldn't concentrate on writing the article, at least I could write thank-you notes; short of that I could make a list of those needing to be written; at least I could write out a rent check. Caretaking and sleeping wasn't all I could do. But one afternoon exhaustion overtook me, and, embarrassed to stretch out on my bed which was next to the crib in which Toni was tending to Ben, I lay down on the floor under my desk, hoping she wouldn't see me. I thought of what a good baby I'd be, how appreciatively I'd remark on each act performed for me. Ben I could kiss a hundred times and he didn't know. I didn't mind the not kissing back as much as the not knowing. I would know if someone kissed me that many times. I'd kiss the hands of anyone who would come and scoop me up and tuck me in . . .

A phone call woke me. It was Jean, the woman in our Lamaze class who had agreed to host our reunion. She gave me the date and time, told me she had a girl, and then asked, tentatively, "How're you doing?"

"Miserably," I said, choking back tears.

"Thank God," she said, "me too. Everyone else I called said they were doing fine."

"They lie. Let's get together."

"How about tomorrow?"

The next morning I dressed Ben in real clothes, not stretchies (the one-piece terrycloth garments babies wear day and night) for the first time, and forced myself into a pair of regular jeans and a not-too-flattering sweater to welcome Jean and her daughter Emily at eleven-thirty.

"What a head of hair!" Jean said, greeting Benjamin. That was what everyone said about his most obviously remarkable feature, which he had had since birth. I always felt like replying, "That's the least of it." Introducing Ben to our new friends, I saw my son assume a reality which until now he'd sustained only in pictures. But here he was, the sum of himself, a whole, permanent human being—Benjamin. And here I was, out of the bedroom at last.

So dazed was I to be with someone I actually liked, who wanted to talk about the same things that I did, who had had similar experiences, that I never got around to offering lunch. We simply sat, talked, and stared at each other's children. I was astonished to see how different they were. Ben had his own distinctive way of sucking, of clamping down on my nipple with a mad fluttering of his head, and stopping only when he was fully asleep, the milk oozing out of his mouth—drunken Buddha, we called him. Emily had a much more refined style. And as a mother, I was distinct, too. Jean, amazingly, didn't bother keeping track of which breast to begin nursing on, and certainly didn't record the length of the nursing or the contents of each diaper, as I did, in my brown notebook. But on most matters which concerned us, we were closely matched. We were even able to complete sentences for each other. "The books," I began, with despair and anger, the books which were supposed to assure us but which frightened me.

"Forget them," Jean said. "They're written by sadists." She

too found them troublesome. That was reassuring. And she allowed me to return the favor. When she worried about not being completely in love with Emily, I told her what Marian patiently repeated to me time after time—that our lives were in crisis, that crises needn't be negative, that we had to work to separate loving the baby from loving taking care of the baby.

"I'm tired of all this caring," Jean said. I was too tired to agree. We drank more coffee and ate some croissants. "I wish someone would nurse me. Or just let me take a nap."

Together we found a strength neither could muster alone. We resolved to attend a mothers' group which met Tuesday mornings in a neighborhood church, to send for information about classes and programs. "I don't usually go in for this kind of thing," we assured one another, knowing each other so little that everything had to be explicit. But we both knew this was our lifeline. We planned to meet in two days. I felt more hopeful than I had in weeks.

Six weeks after Ben's birth, my obstetrician discharged me from her care, declaring me ready to resume sexual relations. Whatever that meant. I welcomed David's interest even as I feared it. He was careful not to pressure me, but I knew he was waiting, waiting. Would I respond as before? Was there any room to feel like anything except someone's mother?

Sometimes, late at night, nursing Ben, I'd gaze over at David trying valiantly to stay awake, and his face shocked me. Large pores, pimples, hair, coarse red skin; the breath from his nose, his mouth; his thinning hair. The sheer size of his face. Ben's was tiny, perfect. I saw Ben's face—in fact, all of Ben—more than I saw anyone else. After days and days of tending to Ben's genitals I was stunned, as if for the first time, glimpsing David's. They looked gross.

Saturday morning, with the crib an arm's length away from

our bed, I slipped in my diaphragm. My movements felt more agile and deft than they had in ages. We were cautious, anticipating pain, discomfort, but feeling almost none. True, one ear was on Ben, but we did finally make love, oh, it had been months, lifetimes. We dozed in each other's arms. Benjamin stirred. Later for you, kid.

One morning David asked me to arrange for a babysitter the next Sunday afternoon; we needed time alone. The Metropolitan Museum of Art was our choice, a destination we shared with many New Yorkers that day. I wanted to see the new wing of primitive art. Later we went to the Temple of Dendur. The museum was soggy and I was beginning to get the slight eye-achy feeling that museums always give me as we strolled through the period rooms, the rooms of armor, weapons, china, costumes, which are almost always empty.

I honestly don't remember how we got onto the subject of extramarital affairs except that we had been talking about the new depth of our commitment to each other. Suddenly David was speculating about what might happen if he should find himself in the right situation far from home, with a stranger . . . something about blond hair.

We had made love for the first time in three months a mere ten days ago. I was in maternity pants. It was time for Ben's next feeding so my breasts were beginning to leak. On the one hand I wanted to say, "Wait. Give me ten days, I'll make myself beautiful, desirable again." On the other, I thought, "Fuck this—I'm doing everything I can to stay alive and if you want me to work any harder . . . "

But then I realized that he wasn't talking about me, or even about us. I knew that he found me attractive, that he wasn't interested in putting our relationship in the least risk. He was only attempting to preserve a notion that his life wasn't suddenly over, that everything wasn't now entirely predictable. He didn't want me to approve of his having affairs, but instead wanted me to say, "Yes, go ahead, anything is still possible, spontaneity is still a word in our vocabulary." I had no right to deprive him of this.

So I kept calm because I honestly didn't feel all that threatened. I told him that I thought our relationship was strong enough to withstand just about anything. I had fantasies of my own, after all.

David felt grateful, absolved; I felt sage. Toward each other we felt a rush of love. In a few weeks, he'd mention that just talking about affairs seemed to have purged his desire to follow through. But even then we felt relieved enough to have a pastry and tea in a neighborhood café before hopping on the bus back to our son.

On the first day of March I turned thirty. Benjamin was flipping himself over by now, batting at the pieces of tinfoil I hung between the slats in his crib, and eager to begin using his legs. He loved his mobile and music boxes, and sucked his thumb like an expert. In his mechanical swing he studied his favorite rattle—a red and yellow barbell—as if through concentration alone he could raise it. A woman in an elevator remarked on his extraordinary eye contact for a ten-week-old. He was doing everything wonderfully, except sleeping through the night.

"You have to help him," an elderly neighbor explained to me. "When he cries in the early morning, don't go in. He's not really hungry. He wants company. Help him to learn how to comfort himself. He's such a big boy." I'd heard this advice before. Some had decried it as selfish, cruel; others had endorsed it, but none so eloquently as this. Now it made perfect sense.

After only a week of feeble 3:00 A.M. crying, Ben began taking care of himself. And David and I had our first uninterrupted night's sleep.

. . .

"Emily slept through the night beautifully for about a month and then stopped suddenly," Jean warned during one of our walks. "So be prepared." We were on our way to yet another group at which we would feel like outsiders. At one group, mothers talked about sibling rivalry. At another, mothers spread exquisite white blankets before their babies and placed the toys on them as if they were the family jewels. We went to groups in which women discussed the problems they were having with their maids, the problems encountered driving to second homes. Nothing fit us except each other. But at least we were out of the house, walking our weight off, complaining about how late our husbands would come home or how often our babies nursed. We had to talk about these things; it was best we do it with each other.

"I mean, I love her," Jean would say, crossing Broadway.

"Sure," I'd say. "You love them." It still wasn't the kind of love we had expected, the kind celebrated through the centuries. It was the kind of love that made you feel as if your day began when they went to sleep, but which also made you tiptoe into the bedroom at least five times a night just to make sure they were still breathing.

Recently I'd found the notebook in which my mother had recorded data about my infancy: who sent presents, how much formula I'd consumed, illnesses, drugstore expenditures, questions for the doctor: "How often shampoo? Oil on scalp? Keep formula 24 hours in fridge?" Virtually the same questions I jotted down in my brown notebook. They hadn't known any more than I did. Had their love for me been as complicated as mine for Ben?

"But I'm so resentful all the time," Jean went on. "I've never lived like this before." What I hated most was waking up feeling so blue. Too depressed to make coffee, to wash my face. I began most days washing shit out of Ben's sheet. Shit is shit.

"Does he have diarrhea?" Jean asked.

"I'm not sure." As we debated whether consistency or frequency constituted diarrhea, my friends were teaching courses, lunching with deputy commissioners, acquiring agents. I was in the middle of a book I'd begun three months ago, reading two pages a night.

"That's more than I have time for," Jean said.

A journalist friend came to visit and asked, with professional ease, what I had learned so far.

"How much I can sacrifice myself," I said instantly. That was all I could articulate at the moment. To myself I added a secret lesson: Loving seems beyond my capability. All the illusions I had proudly toted around about myself—that I was selfless, nurturant, able to sacrifice without minding—went smash, out the window, a lie, a con, a scam.

"One day soon," my mother-in-law promised, "you'll simply wake up and be in love with him. That's all I can tell you. It just happens."

I could wait, I supposed; what else could I do? While I waited it was best to keep busy. Ben and I muddled through the end of winter, and when the weather became a bit warmer we fell into a pleasant, or at least anxiety-allaying routine. We'd spend the day with Jean and Emily: strolling, eating, nursing. About four in the afternoon we'd head home, stopping at the supermarket to pick up something for dinner. In the next hour Ben and I would play together on the couch. Sometimes I took pictures of him propped up against the cushions, his triple chins making him look like a Soviet official. Sometimes we played Pat-a-cake, and sometimes we simply made funny faces at each other.

One frolicsome afternoon we played a game of anticipation.

I placed Ben's head on my knees, his body stretched out along my thighs, and lifted his head to mine, taking a quick catch breath before saying "Benjamin" and dropping him back down. After a few rounds he stared into my eyes, waiting for me to begin again. He had caught on. A synapse in his brain hooked up; I could virtually hear it click into place as his belly laugh subsided. He wanted to laugh again. Our game was illuminated by his brilliant new awareness. He knew we were playing a game, he knew what would happen next, he knew who I was, and he knew that I knew that he knew.

That's all it took. A tiny door opened and I could see beyond it to all the possible pleasures in store. He had stolen my heart. It was spring at last and I was in love.

7

Months Four to Eight
Emerging Slowly

*T*HE LAST TIME I had checked, David had been right next to me, assuring me that we were in this together, feeling his way around the dark edges of our new life as tentatively as I was. Only he could meet my frightened gaze without turning away when I asked him who was this stranger, this miniature despot who had moved in and taken over. He was a gentle husband, an understanding friend and adamant lover, insisting that we pencil in time each Saturday night for a date. These evenings became the high point of my week. I relished slipping into a dress, putting on my makeup and best of all, stepping out the door. We'd kiss waiting for the elevator, congratulating ourselves for having made our escape— this was as free as we'd be. By the time we reached the lobby the weight of the week ahead had already begun to intervene, a week made all the more difficult by David's more and more conspicuous absence.

It wasn't only work that kept him away, but an unwillingness to take the next step in his relationship with Ben, with our new family. "You know Ben so much better than I do," he would say, when I intimated that he could involve himself with more of Ben's caretaking. He was right. I knew Ben better than anybody. When babysitters came, I was now teacher, not student, instructing them as to which positions Ben preferred, at what temperature he liked his milk. This knowledge, I reminded David, wasn't mystically implanted within me, but acquired through long, hard work. He could do likewise. He could watch me diaper Ben and take notes, which he finally did, in our little brown notebook—twenty-one steps.

Our life was one long conversation about how tiring our days were and how dispiriting it was for David to come home to more work, and a bedraggled wife. I would counter with my own ammunition—the tedium, the minutiae with which I had to contend. "At least you're getting out," I'd conclude; "At least you have only one thing to concentrate on," he'd retort. But in the end he relented, conceding not that I had more to do, but that I had the more distasteful task. As he put it so many times, "I couldn't do what you're doing."

There, I'd won. Or had I? Did he mean that I was a hero, or a chump?

Husbands more than babies were on every mother's mind when our own mothers' group—one Jean and I formed with the help of an organization in the business of linking mothers who wanted to talk—met for the first time, a Thursday morning in late April. Jean's kitchen and foyer were transformed into a stroller parking lot, and in her living room sat a tight knot of eight mothers clutching babies. The leader from the organization had us introduce ourselves and our children, and distributed a list of topics she thought we'd like to discuss at later meetings. Sex after parenthood, that's a good one, everyone snickered. At this meeting the woman thought we'd like to talk about our labors and deliveries.

"Oh God no," one woman shuddered.

"Why is it," asked another, "that my husband can stand to let Jake cry so much longer than I can before going to him?"

And so we were off. Question after question laced with frustration, anger, and bewilderment came streaming out. Why didn't fathers seize more initiative in caring for babies? Of what use was a husband who was only titularly in charge, changing diapers when we said to, not bothering to keep track himself? After all, the mechanical act wasn't what we needed release from—we wanted to be off duty. Even for a half hour.

"David doesn't do anything unless I ask him to," I piped up, "and then he's always grumpy, as if I were putting him out, as if he was doing me a favor tending to his own son."

"At least he does it," one woman said. "My husband won't dream of giving up his Thursday night poker game."

With one exception, every woman in that room was over thirty, some closer to forty; we all had careers in various states of temporary suspension. Until now our husbands had given us every indication that their hearts and politics were in the right place— and here we sat, babies at our breasts, perplexed and hurt and feeling abandoned by husbands who had turned into the kind of men we would never have married in the first place. Where *were* they? Why weren't they in it up to *their* necks as well?

We went on to other topics—nursing, sleeplessness, pediatricians —but always came back to husbands: how they didn't get up for middle-of-the-night feedings any more, or if they did, it was only one night out of many.

I couldn't wait to tell David some of what we had chewed over in group, but he came home in a singularly bad mood. He had work to do, it wasn't getting done, nothing was getting done, everything was upside down. "I feel trapped," he cried, he who was gone for twelve hours a day, "I'm unhappy, I've never been so unhappy."

"*You* feel trapped?" I shouted. "You feel tired? What about *me?*"

"I'm not talking about you, I'm talking about me." All I heard was an accusation, that I wasn't doing enough to make him happy; an invitation to reach out, comfort him too. I tried to explain how drained I felt, how needy, but he cut me off.

"You don't understand," he said, "you don't understand at all."

That's when I slugged him. I simply shut down, clenched my fist, and punched him blindly in the arm out of sheer lack of imagination. He didn't say anything then, and to this day we haven't spoken about it, as if it didn't happen—but it did. And then I think I ran out of the house and down two flights of steps without a key or my coat. When I returned, David was calmly eating the dinner I'd left warming on the stove for him.

"How can you eat?" I shrieked, hysterics reawakened.

"Look," he said, "I have to take care of myself."

We went to bed stony but the worst wasn't over. Saturday morning David announced that he had a conference to attend downtown. I wasn't feeling well, and asked him to stay home. To help me out, to make me a cup of tea. He told me he'd be home by noon. And left.

In tears, I called Marian long distance. Haltingly, feeling terribly disloyal, I leaked the story of David's desertion. "You know," she told me, "the last time I spoke to David on the phone, he complained about not having enough time to play tennis. *Tennis.* Here you are, sounding wound up like a machine someone put too many quarters in, and he's complaining about not playing tennis. You have to tell him what you need him to do."

She made it sound if not easy at least straightforward. I didn't have to cajole him into doing more with tales of how much I was doing, I didn't have to cry, feel apologetic or inadequate. I simply had to tell him, "You do this now. I cannot."

When he returned, we had a long talk. I told him that watching Ben entailed not merely playing with him, for he was no longer a toy but an engaging, inquisitive child already in the world. Being with Ben meant keeping track of him: when he needed feeding, changing, dressing up or down. I told him to learn as much as he'd need to so that he didn't have to ask me any questions about what came next. I wanted time away. Really away.

. . .

Some women in our group must have had similar thrashings out with their husbands, and we were eager to calm the tone of our next meeting, to talk of more practical, mundane issues. But several needed to delve more deeply into problems at home. I was realizing that babies brought more amplification than change; I wasn't really different as much as more of myself, and many of the problems that were coming up were augmented, not created, by pregnancy and childbirth. I was neither qualified nor prepared to deal with such unhappy women in an open forum. Already I felt we were way out of our depth: alliances were forming, tempers flared, snide remarks were exchanged.

The warmer weather saved us. Meeting in the park broke the intensity. Our talk centered on who was sleeping through the night, and the merits of various methods which encouraged babies to do so. We were an unwieldy gaggle of mothers and conveyances, whether sitting or strolling in our block-long parade from one playground to the next. Solitary mothers wheeling babies flocked to us, ready to sit down and talk. "We're a group," we told them gently; "call this number, you can form your own." The city parks seemed full of women who, if not eager to discuss their innermost feelings, were happy to share details—how many hours the baby slept, how many ounces he drank—this endless comparing of notes always engaging at first, full of a certain promise, but eventually dissolving into a lulling boredom.

Our meetings ended around noon when several women had to leave, but the rest of us, who had nothing else to do, went for lunch together, and, timing everything around the babies' naps, shopped and strolled back to the park. One afternoon four of us marched up the promenade in Riverside Park, sat down on the same bench, and whipped out our breasts at our children's simultaneous cries. We began talking about summer plans. "I'll be right here," said Jean, propping up her feet and surveying the river. She didn't sound happy.

The woman who spoke last said simply, "My husband and I are going to Rome for two weeks. Alex will stay with my mother."

No one knew what to say. As if on cue, we all closed our blouses and slowly began walking uptown, each getting off at her street. See you tomorrow when the baby train begins again. I walked the last three blocks alone, trying to imagine how I'd have to change before taking a two-week Italian vacation in a month's time would feel comfortable. Did the woman think her son wouldn't miss her? Did she not care? The thought of spending a night alone with David anywhere—an airport motel—made me cry with longing. But leaving Benjamin was beyond me. I needed to *be* with him, to keep apprised of his new sounds, his new expressions, his naps, his eating, his bowel movements. For better or worse, I'd be staying put, measuring out my feelings of outrage, incredulity, envy.

"We should put odometers on these strollers," I told Jean one afternoon. She shrugged. No mother who was likewise strolling would have been shocked by the number of miles, and those who would have been shocked wouldn't have admitted it. So you walk, you're outside, it's better than working.

At first I complained that tending to Ben, being so firmly anchored in the physical, in someone else's concrete needs, kept me from having intellectual thoughts. But if anything, I had rarely felt so stimulated. The alertness I needed to keep up with Ben exercised a previously untapped part of my mind. I was developing a new kind of attention and focus, adequate to appreciate my son's noble efforts toward autonomy. How could I have known that so many infinitesimal steps had to be mastered before simply moving one knee forward? And this was only the first tiny leg of the journey toward synchronizing other movements and crawling, which itself was only a way station on the road to walking. But how did this happen? What drove him so single-mindedly toward mobility, verticality? Why did I think that his personality was formed the instant he was conceived, and what implications did this have? My obstetrician's difficulties in pinning Ben down to get a fetal heartbeat came back to me. He was on the move even then. Who was he, really?

At times I felt flooded with ideas, hypotheses, proposals, speculations. What I didn't have—and desperately wanted—was someone walking alongside me to share everything with; what I most lacked was a structure, the kind David had—classes, seminars, supervisory groups. My thoughts ran free, unchanneled and unanswered, solving my private version of the mind/body problem, from drool to causality.

Ben and I, sealed in a bubble, were whisked out of time in the sense that I had previously understood it. The present was the future, Ben growing each day, moving toward alertness, cognition, recognition imperceptibly, except that I could perceive it. Spending every minute with him, I could literally watch him learn. "What's new?" friends asked when they phoned. Everything was new, but was this what they called to hear about, how Ben's eyes were a quarter-tone brighter today than yesterday? And even that would have been a metaphor. I couldn't begin to explain how he had changed.

Meanwhile, my present-tense time was mired in a daily sameness which defied the notion of time passing. And I felt trapped— to look ahead or back made me dizzy. So much had happened, would happen. The routine had its comforts even as it isolated me, unhinged me. My new world was that of the street and those who inhabited it, the disabled, the sick, the aged, the unemployed. Fewer in number and stamina than those who fought rush hours and lunch hours, we abandoned the streets to them and emerged when they were safely behind desks. To us, the laundry and the supermarket weren't tasks to be squeezed in en route to someplace else but an end, a goal in themselves.

Usually we traveled in pairs—one sitting in a carriage or wheelchair, and one to push. Those with babies often exchanged knowing glances, but older people acknowledged our bond by freely sharing advice and stories: "He needs a hat, dear." Once, as Ben screamed on a cashier's line, a wizened woman took my arm to say, "Don't push the time away, these are the best days of your life." But the woman accompanying her advised me never to underestimate the pain of teething. Her husband's grandmother had lived to be old enough, at 103, to grow a third set of teeth, and she reported that the pain was worse than anything she had previously endured.

Was she in her second childhood, or Ben in a premature old age? He, after all, startled just as my eighty-five-year-old grandmother did upon awakening from a nap or after a fall, both unfurling their hands in a pathetic gesture of self-defense, all they had against the frightening world of sudden consciousness, of hard, sharp surfaces. Toothless, they both gummed their food and twisted their elastic lips. They both needed to involve others in their bodily needs. From the perspective of caretakers—whether of the very young or very old—adulthood, with its accompanying desires for privacy, discretion, and propriety, becomes a fleeting, indulgent moment, a big splash for a while but destined not to last, like a toy jealously guarded only to be finally surrendered.

One day I met a man who recognized me after twenty years; we had been in the same sixth-grade class. We chatted. He was a writer, a teacher—we'd just finished reading the same book. But he was in a hurry, between appointments. He wasn't married, he was having troubles with intimacy, he told me, dashing for a bus. "Let's get together, I'll call you," he shouted. I was flattered by his remembering me and his attentions. We had so much in common, yet because he didn't have a baby, it wasn't enough. How ironic that the glances I exchanged with total strangers toting children were laced with an unmerited empathy, one that arose automatically and quite against my will.

In one moment Ben's eyelids, tinted a translucent lavender by his delicate veins, would blink, and he'd be an adult, taking care of me. Blink—he's old, strapped into a vehicle, someone not yet born, years from being conceived, taking care of him. These were comforting musings; I was at home here, contemplating the reach of generations behind and ahead which I could glimpse in the texture of Ben's now perfect skin and in my grandmother's wrinkles, the compilation of genetic workings more intricate than I could possibly consider, on my daily walk to Riverside Park and back home.

These ruminations led me out of conversational range with many friends. Most, generous in their patience, intuited that I needed time to get back to them. But one, an old friend, a former roommate, couldn't wait and I lost her. I'm sure she has her side of the story, but to me it was a classic case of the baby becoming a threatening measure of where, on an objective and rigid life-plan, I was and she wasn't. She visited me only once during my pregnancy, a week before delivery, to tell me my face looked swollen. She came to the hospital once with flowers and kept repeating, "I can't believe you have a baby." But that was what everyone said—even me. How was I supposed to know that she meant it literally?

After the baby was home, she called to suggest we have a late dinner out, and seemed upset to learn that I couldn't come and go as I pleased. When I tried to explain, she said, "I have to get up early too, you know. I have a hard job, too. At least you have a companion."

Did she mean Benjamin? Her dog was more responsive than my three-month-old son. And when was the last time she had to plan a trip to the bathroom in advance?

In fairness, she wasn't the only one who exasperated me.

Other friends attempted empathy by saying, "I know what it must be like for you. I'm finishing my dissertation," or, "I'm working nights." Having a baby is nothing like doing any of those, I railed silently. Why couldn't they simply acknowledge the difference, the disparity between other life challenges and this particular one? I wanted my uniqueness accentuated, not obliterated. But I knew these comparisons were motivated by good intentions, which were so clearly absent from my other friend's refusal to hear me.

In the end, no longer trusting myself on the phone to refrain from lapsing into our queen-for-a-day routine, I wrote her a letter which explained how needy I felt. If she couldn't attend to this, then our friendship was over. The words came not easily, not without sadness, but with a conviction that surprised me.

Mother's Day, a holiday I used to celebrate by petulantly asking my parents why there wasn't a children's day, was fast approaching. This year, knowing from the inside out that every day is children's day, I finally had something genuine to say to my mother.

I couldn't thank her without trivializing the magnitude of what she had done for me. Long ago, in my angry adolescent diaries, I'd realized that parents can't expect thanks. I was thanking my mother by being Ben's mother. All I wanted to say to her was, I Know. Even though I really knew only about four months' worth of the course she'd been enrolled in for more than thirty years. And still she came over each week to help me out, to do my hand wash, offer money, bring diapers.

Did she remember when I was an infant in her arms; did she remember holding me? Where, in our present-day feelings about each other, were these early memories embedded? How did they come to bear? "I'm finished being a mother," a friend of my mother-in-law announced the summer I was pregnant. I was angry, shocked—how dare she? Even as the new mother in me was beginning to understand, the child in me hoped my own mother would never voice such subversive ideas. She never talked about her own ambivalence; only once when I pushed her did she admit to despair when my father would go to work on Saturday mornings. I nodded knowingly before catching myself. Wait, the child she had dreaded spending time with was me—*me.* I had encroached on her independence, her identity. Was I ready to hear more?

But she hadn't any more to say. She was sorry to see me struggling yet knew my growing pains vindicated her. She was in an enviable position, knowing that I now knew what she had been called upon to give. And my newfound sensitivity to her side of the story worked retroactively. It didn't entirely make up for past hurts or dissolve angry words, and it wouldn't prevent future arguments, but it did imbue our relationship with a loving consideration and an appreciation previously absent.

This was my Mother's Day too, my first, and I wanted it to be special. We spent the afternoon at David's parents' home sorting through suitcases full of old pictures to prove that Ben looked exactly as David did at his age. David disappeared for a few moments, and returned with a small envelope out of which tumbled a strand of pearls, uniformly lustrous, with a white gold clasp.

We stood at the mirror together, David behind me, fastening the necklace. It was the perfect gift, a perfect moment. With my eyes I forgave David all his lapses, apologized for my crankiness of the past months. I hadn't been the only one making sacrifices, after all; David needed understanding as much as I did.

It was peculiar, though, and a bit mortifying how much the pearls meant to me. I'd never been one to concentrate on the inside of a gift box—the card, the intent much more important. But this spring I needed something concrete, something to heft in my palm. I had always been curious about the experience of taking care of someone and I jealously guarded my maternal prerogatives even though in the end the experience nearly overwhelmed me and left me sounding self-righteous when I said nothing could be construed as a pay-back. Frankly, David could take Benjamin for the rest of his life, change every future diaper, sweat out each night Ben asks for the car keys, and nothing would make up for the three months I'd spent with Ben alone in our apartment. Yet I wouldn't have let anyone else take my place.

June brought hints of a returning social life. I celebrated Beth's thirtieth birthday with her and a friend at an intimate afternoon wine-tasting from which I returned delightfully tipsy in time to nurse Ben. We had a wedding to attend, an excuse to splurge on a new dress. David insisted on an exclusive store, money no object, and for once I didn't put up much of a fight. This could be the dress that would catch in Ben's memory, the dress whose texture he would recall as I do my mother's short-sleeved, straight-skirted red and black silk shirtwaist which she wore with black velvet high-heeled open-toed pumps. I know what shade of glossy lipstick she applied and how she combed her hair, parted on the left. I can trace my preference for metal watchbands back to the one my father wore years ago, and never since. The memory gets snagged on these inconsequential, sensual details, these accidents of fads and taste, which become emblazoned, immortalized in a child's mind. One morning my mother, angry at who knows what, raged at me that I was old enough to close the bathroom door, wasn't I, and this rage has become a permanent fixture in my psyche. I was guiltless, of course, but so was she— no one can watch a mood every minute, or react appropriately to each moment's tableau. A parent can't be responsible for every effect she has because everything has an effect. I will do plenty of unthinking things to Ben which he will cart around and dump out in someone's lap, I'm sure; the least I could now do was choose an elegant linen dress with open, wide lapels to show off my neck, and tan mid-high heels to accent my calves.

. . .

As if he knew that in a few days we'd pack up and head for Massachusetts for the summer, Ben concentrated all of his considerable energies in standing upright. Just a few days after he was five months old, he succeeded in pulling himself up in his crib. We heard his triumphant crow and hurried in. The summer boded well. The next six months looked so much easier than the last five, the kernel of hardness surrounding his birth buried in a past becoming ever more remote.

I met Jean and her daughter in the park the day before we left. She brought a gift for Ben and I gave her a card I'd written which said something about her having saved my life. Now I faced two months without her, without our daily consultations, our comforting routines.

My hesitance about leaving took me off guard. Ben's room once felt like a prison—why was I lingering there, memorizing the slant of light through the curtains, during my last night of nursing on the rocking chair? When we returned he'd be eight months old, a different child. I'd have to learn to share him in the months ahead not only with David, who was happily eager to be home with his son, but with David's parents. The prospect of relief from some of my duties was tantalizing. Yet for my free time I'd be trading my exclusivity with Ben. The fragile peace he and I had painstakingly constructed would need remodeling according to new specifications, taking into account new people. We were opening ourselves up.

As we finally drove north, what I felt was relief at putting two hundred miles and three hours between me and the hardest half-year of my life.

Summer in Hinsdale was as the others before Benjamin, the days all similar enough to be parts of one long day, the nights one cool dark draught of sleep. Ben had his own room and his aunt's crib; he adjusted quickly to the new environment and the ministrations of his grandparents. The outdoors beckoned him endlessly, as did the house: three levels, decks and porches, stairs. No wonder he was crawling after only four days, on Independence Day, almost as if he was only waiting until he was sure he had enough space.

In a sense, Ben needed us less now than he needed chairs, sofas, railings. It seemed as if he perceived the world as a series of ledges upon which to hoist himself. His grandmother called him Sherpa Baby. Like an indomitable, solitary climber, he worked alone through his first summer, achieving, by its end, when he was just seven months old, two, sometimes three solo steps.

I was freer than I'd been since before his birth. His grandparents and father were happy to give him bottles of formula, to feed him solids in his new highchair. When we visited with friends, he easily came along—in a pack on my back, in his car seat or stroller. Not many people my age summer with their parents, and while there were some problems, in the end everyone was served. David and I had a sweet interlude of time together, to take tennis lessons, resume running and writing, to attend plays, movies, dinners out; and David's parents took a giant step into grandparenthood. My father-in-law especially savored his role, reminding me frequently that he hadn't had this chance to see his own children grow up before his eyes, working nights and going to school by day.

And what a delight Benjamin was to watch grow. "He's just like his father," my mother-in-law would say, relating another story of David's infancy or childhood. I loved the stories. David as a baby, Benjamin as a thirty-year-old father. What kind of relationship would I have with Ben in thirty years?

One night we were bathing Ben in his little tub on the kitchen counter, a time his grandmother and I particularly enjoyed, admiring anew each night his eyelashes lengthened and separated by the water, his glistening skin. I still loved him naked best of all. "It will be so strange not to have access to his body in a few years," I said, so familiar was I now with its every pore.

"That's okay," Phyllis said. "By the time that happens it's time enough."

Then, while I dried Benjamin off, she and Marvin dumped the bath water, rinsed the tub, washed out the milk bottles and refilled them, replaced the shampoo and soap away, so that when I came out of the bedroom having nursed Ben to sleep everything was put away, ready for tomorrow night. They also did the bulk of the shopping, house managing, budgeting, like busy stagehands scurrying around behind the scenes so that my new family could be given star treatment. Only when I saw four adults kept entirely busy by Benjamin did I realize what I had accomplished in seven months—not only making peace with myself, my son, and my husband, but handling all the scut work as well. How in the world had I done it for the first half of Ben's life? How would I be ready to assume all these duties again, when summer was over?

Late August was the best time for spending twilight on the float —the lake free of bugs and all varieties of human noise. I spent many evenings there alone, flat out on my back, arms spread apart, palms up, feet slightly separated, in the yoga position known as the corpse. I wasn't interested in scenery, but in exposing as much body surface area as possible to the bobbing stillness. Jean once said that the hardest adjustment to motherhood was the fact that you're never alone. Even an infant comes equipped with a host of demands for speech, acknowledgment, like a favorite blanket or teddy. The simple quiet presence of the tiniest child is nonetheless a presence with which to contend. I had felt as though I'd never be alone again.

Yoga had taught me to imagine myself slipping out of my body on a slim filament of my exhalation, hovering above and observing. Behind me was the house, revealed in an instant for what it was: a container for human interaction. Lit up and humming, it glowed not only from the sound of radios, televisions, and dishwashers, but with the friction of competing emotions. It was home, both physically and spiritually. There was no real running away, only these moments of concentrated solitude.

Last year, when I'd rested here, I'd imagined that Ben would be with me. I wanted this experience of the lake and sky to be interwoven with his earliest remembrances. What I hadn't counted on was the benefit—the blessing—of his early bedtime. Now I wasn't about to wake him. This had been only his first summer, there'd be plenty more, plenty of time in which to hold him on my lap, or drape my arm along his shoulders, draw him close, and explore with him the pleasures of finding peace in the falling darkness.

8

Months Nine to Twelve
First Steps

THE LAST DAY of summer began at six-thirty with Ben crying. "Maybe he's not getting enough milk," David suggested, walking into the room where I was trying to nurse Ben as I had every morning for eight and a half months. "Maybe you're dried up."

His tone was gentle even if his choice of words wasn't. Glumly I made Ben a bottle which he snatched and downed. At night I tried once more. After tears at the breast, he chug-a-lugged the bottle and bounded off to sleep.

"He's weaned, I suppose," I admitted sadly the next day as we drove back to the city. Neither David nor I knew why I was sounding this way. Some sadness was appropriate for the end of an era. But nursing had never been my favorite part of motherhood; in fact, I'd been planning to wean Ben by precisely this time. In two days I had to return to work and the notion of expressing milk into bottles to be sterilized, frozen, and dated seemed like the last thing a nervous, newly working mother needed to fuss with.

Maybe I was feeling guilty about not feeling guiltier. In fact, I was liberated, no longer singled out for special service. Anyone could give Ben a bottle and, contrary to pro-nursing propagandists, whose every word I remembered even as I dismissed them, bottles could be given warmly, lovingly, while cradling and cooing to the child. I could buy regular bras, my breasts would go back to their regular size. I wouldn't have to worry about making it home in time for feedings, or about Ben having his fill before my supply was drained. If he didn't finish a bottle, I didn't care. So why was I girding myself with arguments against unvoiced assailants, as if implicitly accused of blasphemy?

My judges were those overzealous women only too eager to tell me that nursing was the most satisfying experience of their lives. I never entirely believed them. Nursing was certainly profound but not complex; deep but not broad. After several thousand nursings, how many unexplored angles could remain?

Yet my stance was faintly heretical even to me, and I had trouble confessing to my closest friends, all of whom seemed to find in nursing something I didn't. I felt privileged to have nursed Ben for eight months, though I may have persisted a bit longer than I cared to, hoping to see the light. If I have another child, I'll nurse again. And if these were my feelings then they were valid, not substandard feelings; they didn't necessarily bespeak inadequacy on my part, or worse.

Nursing is too charged an issue these days, I concluded, too bound up in women's self-esteem, worth, and adequacy to occasion rational discussion. After all, maybe I was upset simply because I loved the bedtime feedings, when watching his eyes close seemed as much a miracle as watching them open, and I wished my body could have granted us just a few more.

Ben tolerated the drive home very well, sleeping until we stopped for lunch at my aunt's, where he scooted around the house like a human rocket bent on winning hearts. "What a personality on him!" my uncle exclaimed. He unfurled our family tree to show us the spot where Ben's name had been recently inscribed, and the spot he was saving for his own grandson, due in a month. A few branches back I saw my mother's uncle Ben whom I well remember, a roly-poly white-haired, gentle, smiling man, who always came to visit with treats and kindness. My sister maintained that my Benjamin resembled him. Uncle Ben had run away from his home in Latvia, unwilling to serve in the Czar's army. All the details of his life were a romantic blur to me. But at least I'd heard him speak Yiddish, at least I'd known him. To my son, his namesake would be only a figure in a snapshot, awkwardly posed and silent.

On the last leg of our journey, David and I sang ourselves hoarse trying to keep Mr. Personality amused. We could barely hear, much less keep track of, the baseball game on the radio which we always listened to on the Labor Day ride home. As stubborn as our child, we stayed tuned in, a ceremonial gesture reminding us that our previous five homecomings weren't like this one. Usually we double-parked, left all our gear unpacked in the middle of the living room, checked in with friends, shared a pizza, and stayed up late. Tonight we parked, unpacked immediately to find Ben's things to keep him on schedule, gave him supper and a bath, put him to bed, and soon fell asleep ourselves. Welcome home.

My task before my teaching job began was to find a babysitter. Although Ben would be attending an infant-care program two afternoons a week, I needed someone in the house with him once a week. Friends of friends didn't work out; neither did the college service with which I enrolled. My leads were soon exhausted. What now?

"Put me down in a foreign country in the middle of the night with another country's currency," Jean often said, "and I'd land on my feet. But ask me to find a competent babysitter for my daughter . . . " We felt equally lost. If we had known about what routinely went on in the parks—good babysitters spotted, lured into conversation about salary, wooed away with promises of more money, more free time—we would have been even more dispirited.

Complicating my task was Ben's separation anxiety and my own. He wailed as soon as I left his sight; I was slower to acknowledge my dread at leaving him, though it nearly made me physically

sick. I wished I could sneak out when he wasn't looking, as someone suggested. Instead, I made him take it on the chin: "Mommy
has to leave now, I know you're unhappy, but I'll be back very
soon"—this recitation for my benefit more than his. I knew he had
to cry. He was unhappy. I couldn't very well ask for approbation
and understanding from a nine-month-old, could I?

The force of Ben's need for me took me aback. After months
of not seeming to care about my whereabouts, he turned exclusively to me for comfort. My body, its folds, surfaces, enclosures,
quieted him as nothing else did. The hours I'd spent worrying that
we'd never bonded, that he somehow sensed my ambivalence and
rejected me, seemed like so much wasted time. Here was his will
I had so longed to sense, and his list of personal needs. His blank
slate was being filled with faint letters, and they seemed to spell
Mama.

While we were looking for a regular sitter, I called the agency we
had used when Ben was an infant. One afternoon a tall, athletic-
looking woman showed up at my door talking. She never stopped.
She paid only peripheral attention to Ben, but I assumed she was
intent on impressing me while I was still around. I left, because I
had to, with vague misgivings, and ended up phoning David at his
office to ask him to check in on Ben in about an hour.

Three hours later when I returned, David was washing typewriter ribbon ink off Ben's fingers, the curtains on the French doors
were torn down, every toy was piled on the living room rug. The
girl was in the kitchen making herself a cup of tea. "Pay her,"
David growled, "and get her out of here."

She left; I felt as if I should have been arrested. How could I
have left my son in those utterly incompetent hands? "You have
to find someone reliable," David said. This wasn't the time to
disabuse him of the notion that only mothers are responsible for
finding sitters—he had to leave for class and I had to come up with

a plan. First, I called the agency to complain. The woman acted surprised that I hadn't been charmed by her employee. I told her to expect no further calls from me or any of my acquaintances. Next, I frantically called every other agency I could find listed, knowing that I'd never use one again. I was marking time until I felt recovered enough to pack Ben in his stroller and set out for the college of education in our neighborhood, index card, Magic Marker, and thumbtack in my bag.

There I intercepted a high school girl putting up a sign of her own. Seizing the moment, I interviewed her on a bench in the lobby; that is, I asked her inane questions so she wouldn't notice how hard I was scrutinizing her. She was clean, deferential, pretty, sane, a student at a fancy private high school, a neighbor. She agreed to come over and meet Ben before starting and promised letters of reference. "Three fifty an hour all right?" I asked. My offer was probably a dollar or so higher than she would have requested had I let her speak. "Sure," she stammered.

She came regularly, every Tuesday afternoon, to give Ben dinner and put him to bed. The one time she was sick, she gave me the name of a friend who could substitute. She always told me how cute Ben was, and that he ate all of his dinner and never cried. For the first few weeks, I looked in the garbage to see if she was lying, but either she was right or a scrupulous cleaner. As soon as she left, I'd tiptoe into Ben's room where he was always sleeping peacefully. If he had cried at all, it couldn't have been for very long.

This is how Tuesdays ran in our house that semester. We awoke at seven after a restless night worrying about how the day would unfold. David left forty-five minutes later for a class and returned at noon, by which time I had changed into teaching clothes, eaten lunch, prepared lunch and dinner for Ben and dinner for us, and was ready to leave. At five the babysitter came to relieve David, who left for a seminar. I returned at eight, David at nine, when we had dinner. It wasn't so much a day to get through as a series of interlocking obstacles. When something went wrong—anything, a stuck elevator, no change for the bus—the whole day was thrown off and I was left feeling as if the avalanche of mundanities to which I had to attend was snuffing the life out of me. But when things went right—the weather clement, subways on time—if no one got sick or had to go away on a class trip, if the wash and shopping had been done, then Tuesday was a thing of beauty, an elaborate, intricate mechanism requiring wit, skill, and wisdom for its masterful execution. And best of all, it found me, when I closed the door to my apartment at noon, free.

Free to teach two classes. Have office hours. To eat a snack on the literal run to my next class, and then scrounge for a taxi during the worst hours (a would-be luxury turned into another chore) to get home in time to pay the babysitter and send her home. Only a fool would call this freedom, but I was unaccompanied and dressed attractively on Madison Avenue, carrying a briefcase, not pushing a stroller, engaged in conversations about politics and language, not formula and diapers. By the time I returned home, the lights were dim, the baby fed and asleep and beyond needing me.

Wednesday morning I'd be Mom again, in grubby clothes down on the floor with Ben, on the phone with Jean, back in the mothers' network. Thursdays I straddled both worlds, meeting with my group in the morning, rushing home at noon to change clothes and leaving to teach my class, Ben's cries fresh in my ears.

One afternoon, on my way to the bus stop, I passed the outdoor café where Rita and Jean, their children asleep in their strollers, were lunching. For a moment I contemplated sitting down with them. Then I wouldn't have to worry about the bus arriving on time or my class succeeding; I could dismiss the babysitter, comfort Ben, and take a deep breath. We'd all drink coffee, wait for the kids to nap again, and finally decide whether to walk down the east or west side of Broadway.

I quickened my step. I'd take the anxiety, the rush, the challenge over the boredom and depression, at least until tomorrow when I'd be home again.

Still, I worried about leaving Ben. Defensively, David and I calculated what percentage of Ben's waking time he was with me alone, with a babysitter, in day care. The numbers were comforting; in fact, it seemed an eminently practical way in which to divvy up time for everyone. But then why was I left feeling, in all the debates that took place among mothers about staying home versus working—in the playground, play groups, elevators, on the phone, obsessively—that I was my only ally, that my views were discounted equally by both camps? I found truth in the wisdom of both staying home and working, but was a traitor to those who did one or the other full time, uncomfortable embracing either one at the expense of the other. Sure, my path had its difficulties. Shifting gears from teaching to mothering and back consumed energy in itself. At times I felt entirely fragmented, one day a runner passing mothers on benches, the next one of the mothers being passed. While everyone else felt compelled to choose, I knew that my recipe for sanity lay in not forcing myself to decide to be a full-time anything, in not blending images of myself, in not allowing one role to overshadow another. Let my closet contain many hats, or at least two or three. I'd never be happy with just one no matter how perfect the fit.

Once it had been reasonable for me to define myself by what I did, but not now. Motherhood took up too much time and concentration. It could lull an unsuspecting person into thinking that this was all she did, all she was. To preserve a notion of a former self, a woman has to rise above her circumstances, and she can't do it alone. At least I couldn't. David helped. We still went out on Saturday night dates. As important as it was for him to be a father, he had to think of himself as a husband and of me as a friend, a wife.

And friends helped, too. Beth, for one, took on the responsibility for seeing to my personal social life. She made plans for us to have dinner together, go to movies, or just get together as we used to before the baby. She asked about Ben but made clear that to her he was only another part of my life. Her primary interest was me.

Other friends had more difficulty figuring out how to deal with me. They sensed that my grace period was over, my credit used up, that with a return to relative stability within my immediate family, it was time to consider relationships in the next concentric circle outward.

One friend called to invite us to dinner on a Friday night at about seven, precisely the time Ben went to sleep. Even if I had wanted to find a babysitter, I wouldn't have been able to succeed on such short notice. "Bring him," she said. "Everyone wants to see him."

I was being set up. Neither Ben nor I would have fun if he came along. He wasn't a plaything but someone with whom I had to live, whose schedule I had to respect so he would respect mine. How could I enjoy myself to the background music of his crankiness?

"All I know is that when I have a child . . ." my friend began, she'd follow the footsteps of those more intrepid parents she knew who thought nothing of packing up their children, some even younger than Ben, and marching off to concerts or antinuclear rallies, not to mention mild dinner parties.

But I had stopped listening. I heard my mother's voice in mine when I said to myself, "I don't care what you think you'll do or what anyone else does. This is what I do. And you, my friend, have no idea of how you'll feel when the baby is yours."

"You can't cut off your social life," she went on. "You have needs too." No one had to tell me about my needs, thank you. I was all too aware of them, bunked my head on them every time I stretched. And high on my list was the need to stay home on Friday nights, eat a somnambulant dinner with David, and crawl into bed by nine. One of the last things I needed was to drink to a lifestyle from which I was apparently exiled.

The day-care center which so tantalized Ben—its clear expanse, its toys, the walking and talking older children—urged parents to remain with their children during the first few difficult weeks. David and I took turns accompanying Ben to his two afternoon sessions and met other parents who felt similarly exiled from huge chunks of adult life. I was as eager to make new friends as a schoolgirl.

In the room which looked as if a huge machine had descended through the ceiling and compressed all the furnishings to knee level, we chatted, compared notes, and watched these little people accustom themselves to each other and a new environment. I felt almost as awed as an anthropologist stumbling upon a remote, perfect society in which my son had a definite role completely unknown to and independent of me.

He seemed to adjust quickly, and after a few weeks, as other parents began disappearing, I brought Ben over at two o'clock in my running clothes. My game plan for the afternoon was to run, shower, read the paper, and drink iced coffee until five-thirty. But Ben began crying so bitterly when he saw me leaving that I said I'd stop by after my run to make sure he'd calmed down.

Forty-five minutes later he met me in the lobby in the arms of a teacher. "I think you'd better stay," she said, "at least for a few hours."

I sat in the corner, on cushions, fuming and guilt-ridden. Ben, of course, instantly recovered and proceeded to ignore me for the rest of the afternoon except for brief glances to make sure I was still captive. Many of the other children whose parents had left looked forlorn, dispirited, abandoned. I wouldn't want Ben to be that unhappy, I thought, yet I envied their parents for being away. They must have had real-world commitments whereas I had only my wish to have a single free afternoon. But sure, I'd sit and watch kids run around a room supervised by professionals whose salaries I was underwriting with a sizable tuition payment. Swell.

What if I really had to teach this afternoon? Would I have been able to leave him?

The head teacher must have noticed my agitation, for she came over during snack to explain that it often takes longer than we'd like for children to acclimate. "He's very little," she said, "and he's only here eight hours a week."

How could she, a stranger, have compassion for Ben's best interests and leave me, his mother, to bask in selfish anger? She hadn't meant to shame me, of course, but I blushed. "Why don't you bring some work to do here," she suggested. Then she moved Ben's stroller into the room with him, and told us to bring other items from home. Ben appreciated these touches, and selected for the occasion his most beautiful stuffed animal—Panda.

About three weeks later, I looked up from my crossword puzzle to see Ben completely absorbed in an activity and had the sense that if I left he would be fine. The teacher agreed. I kissed him goodbye and walked outside. He cried but stopped after only a few moments. I know, because I waited right outside the door. And then I tiptoed home to spend a few solitary hours which were no less sweet for their belatedness. In fact, the time went slowly, and I found myself back at the center fifteen minutes earlier than I had to be.

I opened the door slowly, peeking in hoping to glimpse what was taking place unobserved. All the children were seated at the table having snack and among them, incredibly, was Ben. Just one of the kids, perhaps a bit more wriggly and unsteady, but one of a group, a participant, someone's peer. One of his friends saw me and said immediately, "Ben Mama." Then Ben's body turned toward me, as if beyond his will he were programmed to search me out, and he ran toward me, fell down, crawled backward, and let out a war whoop in a crazy dance of excitement. These were lovely moments, lovely to watch as well. "Mama, you came back." I'll prove it over and over again.

Sometimes, of course, Ben or one of his friends greeted an anxious returning parent with implacable indifference. "That means they're angry, right?" I asked David. His response was multi-faceted: there was no way to know, don't ascribe your own feelings to your child, children are entitled to as full a spectrum of feeling as any adult. I trusted David; he spent full afternoons at the center with Ben out of pure interest, got to know all the children well, and came home with the best stories. One afternoon, a talkative two-and-a-half-year-old girl approached David. Holding out her fist, she said something that sounded like "Soul brother." David took one look at her intent gaze, her neat braids close to her scalp, and extended his own hand. "Soul brother," he said solemnly.

"I used to have a boo-boo here," she explained, "but now it's s'all brotter."

Not every story from this period of Ben's life left us laughing. After enjoying perfect health for nearly ten months, my antibodies left Ben flat and he was sick suddenly, frighteningly, running a temperature of 104.5 at eleven o'clock at night, an intimation of the long corridor of horrors ahead. The doctor told us how to cool and comfort him. A few days later, Ben woke up early, whimpering, with a liquidy discharge coming out of his left ear. I jumped in a taxi and sped to the doctor's, who scooped out Ben's infected ear, gave me a prescription for penicillin, and assured me, after I mentioned that Ben had never been so listless, "Don't worry, I've seen much worse."

Worse? All afternoon, as I tried to figure out how to get the thick pink medicine into Ben's mouth, as I marveled at how I had managed to find a taxi, get to the drugstore, and back home, I wondered how I would ever cope with a situation worse than this one: Ben seemed drained of life itself. But a few doses of the syrup had him better quickly. We spent the next two days indoors—unmercifully, impossibly long days—which, after twenty-five years, hadn't changed at all from the ones I remembered when the convalescent was me.

On a Thursday morning, just a week after his nine-month birthday, Ben pulled himself to standing against a stool in the kitchen and paraded out, by himself. I was on the phone with an operator, who said, "Excuse me, ma'am?" when I exclaimed, "Oh my God, he's *walking!*"

It was a season of firsts: first haircut, first shoes, first snowsuit. First bloody fall, against a piano bench. In my panic I called the doctor immediately, not realizing that I wouldn't be able to hear a word with Ben screaming in my ear. "Calm down," the doctor shouted. Believe me, I was trying.

There was an important first for David and me. We left Ben at my parents' one Saturday afternoon, and drove to Montauk, alone. Shy, as if surprised to find ourselves in the car alone, delighted, for traveling was one of the things we did best together, we drove straight to the Point for a late afternoon lookaround out to sea. Our motel faced the ocean. We took a walk on the beach, ate a leisurely dinner, and phoned my mother only once to make sure that Ben went off to sleep without trouble so that we could, too.

In the morning I had a craving for an early run on the beach, a huge breakfast, and the Sunday papers. We felt weightless, almost giddy. How was it possible that life was once like this? On the way back we stopped at a bookstore to buy Ben a present. For a moment he seemed entirely remote, all my time with David, all my years alone tipping the scale, Ben but an instant, a minuscule fraction of my life. David and I had spent so many days ambling through stores, new towns, restaurants, decisions, as we were now. I had missed my husband more than I'd realized. The loss of our comfortable day-to-day life with only each other remained the hardest loss to reconcile.

We stayed late and had to speed back to my mother's. I concentrated on compressing every lovely, sunlit detail into a tiny charm to store in my pocket and finger as needed. "Time, time, time is on my side, yes it is," sang the Rolling Stones.

Ben, shy with us for about ten seconds, broke into grins and paroxysms of joy. He loved his new book, knew how to turn the pages, and freely expressed the rejuvenation we were all feeling. Maybe next time I'd be away long enough to miss him.

In November, we decided to have a dinner for the mothers and fathers of those still in our mothers' group—no babies please. We each made a dish and met at Jean's house to find that we had all dressed up a bit—makeup, jewelry, shawls. Nobly, we attempted conversation but found, by the time Jean served her roast, that the children were all we had in common and cared to talk about. Jean's husband began to explain his daughter's eating habits: "Two kernels of corn is a meal for Emily," but Jean cut him off. "Dear," she said, "these women know how Emily eats. They have lunch with her three times a week." What she meant was, they may even know her habits better than you do.

And perhaps it was at that moment that the evening changed its tenor. The men were strangers to each other, and the five women hadn't known each other for even a year, but we were bonded together as soldiers in the trenches. We told stories of the old days, the early days, laughing to the point of crying—the laugh of the battle fatigued, the kind of laughter that makes you shiver, cry, as you do leaving a hospital or a funeral, that arises from a biological need for release. We had survived more than we ever imagined we could, had learned more about our instincts for survival, our capacities for both love and resentment than we had perhaps bargained for; the sources of our joy and our anguish had never been so completely fused and inseparable.

By eleven we came to our senses, got our coats, and kissed each other goodnight: it was already late, a matter of moments before we had to wake up again. We promised we'd do this again soon, but somehow we never did.

The approaching holidays were eclipsed by prospect of our children turning one. Jean gave me the idea for a birthday letter. She wanted to write to Emily, she said, to tell her about their first year together. "But when will she be able to read it?" she asked. "When she's eighteen? Twenty-one?"

"Who knows," I said, envisioning the tender moment when I would give Ben the packet I had been keeping for him of all the letters I had written to him each year, on his birthday, each sealed and dated. I wished the idea had originated with me, but it was too good not to borrow.

I began early, luckily, for the task proved more difficult than I had imagined. My first draft was a mere catalogue of his most recent exploits. He filled and dumped containers, said "Hot" pointing to the radiator, anticipated every page of *Pat the Bunny*. He walked like Frankenstein, and his incipient speech, all propulsive, percussive spits and stutters, came out like sentences. He was learning patience. One morning he waited for us, wide awake, contentedly sucking on his thumb and stroking Panda, knowing we'd come for him eventually so there was really no need to get all hot and bothered.

All these moments were more fodder for a camera, a tape recorder, a movie than for my clumsy words. But I was the most reliable video camera he had, the one focused on him for nearly every moment of his life. Could I remember everything? As much as I loved his walking, I didn't ever want to forget the complicated series of acrobatic rolls by which he had propelled himself on his belly. As eager as I was for him to talk, I didn't want to lose the music of his earliest sounds. He wasn't even a year old and he had discarded selves. Whatever happened to drunken Buddha?

This was the heart of the letter: How had we come to feel a family, not a group of people thrown together but three who fit? If every account of this process I had read glossed over the difficulties, neither had any adequately depicted the wonder, the boundless mystery as thoroughly and profoundly as David and I felt it.

I put the letter aside for a while. The semester was ending, arrangements had to be made anew for the coming term. My cousin's wife had a baby and two friends became pregnant within weeks of each other. I calculated that when these babies were born, Ben would be twenty-one months, the same age that Leah was when Ben was born, when she had plucked a rose from a bouquet brought home from the hospital.

To these friends, I was the authority. One of them began worrying aloud about how she would manage to adjust to childbirth, nursing, and a return to work in a six-week period. "Don't worry," I said, "it's not so bad."

"You liar," she yelled. "You were crazy in the beginning, you were as unhappy as a person could be."

She was right. I hadn't forgotten, and I certainly hadn't wanted to assume the tone of voice I had found so offensive, to be guilty of the thoughtlessness that had so angered me. Without dismissing her very real apprehensions, I wanted only to offer this perspective: With time, the work doesn't become any easier, but the rewards increase beyond measure. By the time your child is twelve months, I wanted to assure her, you find yourself living with a new person, a walker, a communicator, someone who has a will, volition, who wants certain things and not others, someone who craves you. If watched carefully enough, he can shed light on one of the greatest mysteries: how do we learn? He stashes dirty clothes in your file cabinets, climbs into the bathtub with his clothes on, lies down voluntarily for a diaper.

He is the subject of parent-teacher conferences at the day-care center at which you learn how others see him, that he has an unfolding existence when he's not with you, as part of a group. You hear his praises sung. The teacher says, "He's a lucky little boy," and then emends herself: "You're all lucky."

I returned to my letter, thinking I was ready to record the sense of who he was. I began by describing his "imperious finger," as his grandmother called it, pointing to what he wanted—and he wanted everything. He pointed to where he wanted to be taken, insistent on getting more experience, more information. Soon he'd learn the words "I want," but once he had pointed with his head before he found his index finger. I was an archive devoted exclusively to him, I had all the documents in the stacks of my mind waiting for him to request access. And just in case he never did, I'd write these letters. "You were always yourself," I wrote, "from your Lanugo days: you haven't changed, only grown."

From these letters, from what I omitted, stressed, repeated, and altered, Ben would have a sense of his evolving mother as well. I thought of another letter I wanted to write, to my journalist friend, who had in the dead of last winter asked what I had learned from my baby. I had learned the meaning of paradox: I knew my limits and my limitlessness, I had learned that I was both flexible and rigid, that I longed for the future and the past equally, that I was needy and needless, mother and daughter, child and adult, locked in a family and adrift alone.

Many paths may yield this knowledge of self, but I had learned it through my son. For the next eighteen years or so Ben would be home with us, and then he'd go. Eighteen years isn't very long.

Perhaps by the time he's ready to leave, it will seem different; I don't know. My mother and I fought our way through my adolescence, yet when she came home after depositing me at college she had to close the door to my bedroom. Better to imagine me inside, on the phone, resenting her knocks, than really gone.

Ben had two birthday parties, one a small family gathering at our house and then a large, noisy gala at his grandparents'. At both he was transfixed by the candles, stunned by the singing, and more intrigued by the cake, the boxes and wrappings than the presents. David and I meant to take ourselves out to celebrate a year of parenthood, but we never did.

On the eve of Ben's birthday, I sat at my desk with the unfinished letter. I'd filled three pages and needed only a closing. I wanted to write that the best I could wish for him was a child of his own, one day, who would make him as happy as he was making David and me. That's what old people always say, I thought, precisely the kind of sentiment young people dismiss.

There I caught myself. If I let what I wrote be determined by what I thought he'd want to read when he turned eighteen in the shapeless, cloudy future, the letters wouldn't be worth saving. The best I had to offer Ben was my honesty.

I signed the letter, sealed it, and placed it in a box for safekeeping. Then I went into his room to adjust his covers and place his Panda, his beloved Panda, within reach.

9

Epilogue

*M*Y MOTHERS' GROUP meets infrequently these days, more out of nostalgia than need. We long ago exhausted the once provocative list of discussion topics: TV violence, babysitters, sex. Sometimes we consider throwing a communal birthday party since our kids will turn two almost simultaneously, but even as we plan we know it won't pan out. We still exchange tips: all parents do. (Ellen delighted us one morning by telling us how she had suspected two burly workmen trailing her down the subway platform only to hear one say to the other, as they overtook her, "But Pampers without gathers *leak* . . . ") Mostly we watch our children, these remarkably resourceful, independent creatures who amuse themselves with their own games and rituals, needing us only to dispense food and settle territorial disputes, leaving us free to sit on the couch with our coffee and discuss the only topic about which we have high feeling—second children.

We all know each other's positions and state them anew each meeting more for ourselves than anyone else. Ellen, a twin, knows that she wants another child soon. She claims that a sibling relationship is unique, important, that it equalizes the family constellation into two dyads instead of one triad. Kids take care of each other and give the parents more freedom.

"Not for a long time," warns Jean. She has an older stepson and her family will grow no further. "Another person means a new set of needs. I couldn't cope."

"Siblings don't automatically get along," adds Rita, one of

four children herself. She always thought she'd have two children but now she thinks not. "You have to have a second child for you, not for your first child."

That's when they turn to me. What I want to say is, I agree. With everything, both sides, it's all true. But this satisfies no one. "I just don't know," I stammer, when prodded. "As soon as I think no, I couldn't, I wonder if I mean it. If I'm really finished."

Everyone laughs but I am serious. Suddenly the most important consideration is tactile. How can I resign myself to having touched my last babyflesh? Perhaps I'll be relaxed enough to enjoy a second infancy. And imagine the luck of the child who has Ben as an older brother.

Recently David has taken to saying, when people ask, that he thinks we will have another, but in three or four years. ("Fine," I say to myself. "You carry it; you gain forty pounds and you deliver.")

"The longer you wait, the more independent Ben gets, the more disrupted your life will be when a new baby comes," Ellen reminds me. As if I didn't know.

A neighbor in Hinsdale has one child, a seven-year-old boy who kindly adopted Benjamin last summer. His mother and I watched the boys throw stones into the lake and she asked me, in a tone which said, "I know I shouldn't be doing this but I will," if we had thought of having another child. "Sure," I said, "I'd love for Ben to have an older brother or sister." She laughed. Then she told me not to be overly concerned about having only one child. "It gets bad press," she said. She was an only child.

"It's funny," she went on. "You can't wait until they can talk. And when they do, they never ask you the questions you hoped they would, the questions you prepared for: 'Why is the sky blue?' 'What causes wind?' Instead they ask, 'Why is that man wearing a green shirt? Why does that woman laugh so loud?'" She threw up her hands. Down at the shore, Ben began singing a song and Brad picked up the rhythm, danced, whooped, fell down, cracked up.

She must have noticed the look in my eyes. "Don't let that scene fool you for one minute," she said. "They're friends, not brothers." But to me it looked as if her son and mine were freest to be themselves with each other.

My mother calls to ask me if she can give some of Ben's old clothes, which I have stashed in plastic bags in her closets, to her friend's grandson. I hesitate. "You don't save socks, pajamas, undershirts," she says, exasperated. "But I gathered a few bags of usable pants and shirts."

"Will she give them back?" I ask.

"Honestly," she says.

What am I trying to say?

I'm already a parent forever. How can I justify having another child? How can another child David and I have not be Benjamin? If only there were a way to wade into this decision. But now I know about 3:00 A.M. nursings, middle-of-the-night fevers, my own brittle neediness. Maybe this is the best reason to have another: Ben needs someone to deflect our nervous energy; we need some insurance. Anything could happen.

"You have to be careful with a child like Ben," my aunt cautioned, an aunt who has one child. "He's so good, so clever . . . " I know all about it. I was a first child. And my sister made sure I knew her side of the story.

Often, after putting Ben to bed, I stand at my bedroom window eating my supper out of a plastic bowl and stare into a set of windows across the alley where a couple is preparing dinner. First she smooths a white linen tablecloth, then adds blue place mats and napkins. Then she takes the candlesticks from the mantle. Next, wineglasses, flowers, serving pieces. They sit at their table until way past nine. "How can you not have children?" I rail at them. "What's the *matter* with you?"

In a calmer moment I can admit that elegance in this vein was never our style, that even before Benjamin our meals were informal at best. But now I can no longer amuse myself by thinking that one day this kind of life could be mine. My house will always be cluttered, my clothes sometimes stained, mealtime a raucous occasion. I'd already bought a vinyl tablecloth, plastic bowls and cups. Could a second child take me any farther from the life I glimpse across the way?

Benjamin at twenty-two months is a conversationalist. He is witty, knows a good joke when he hears one, recites nursery rhymes, makes up puns and analogies. At the doctor's office, to which he and I will make only two scheduled visits during his third year, we will meet mothers of six-week-olds, three-month-olds. They will study Ben cavorting in the waiting room—playing his imaginary guitar, sliding backward down the slide, reading books, showing off his extensive vocabulary—and one will say to me in a whiny, desperate voice, "He's so *cute*," as if hers turned more lumpen by comparison. I sounded like that too, not long ago. But now all I'll want to say is, "Wait, listen to this," as Ben takes a deep breath and goes for an extra syllable, stringing together longer and more complex units of speech with unparalleled bravery and daring—"Did you hear that?" His every sibilant and lisp a wonder.

Ben has enriched our lives in every way that David and I suspected and hoped having a child would. "Enrich" is a pale word to describe the transformation he brought. Because of his existence we have had to adjust our vision so profoundly that we see nothing as we did before. It's as if he taught us a new, more complete language which makes all others wooden stammerings; it's his light which illumines the dark corners into which we had never thought to peer. Day after day he turns our lives inside out, brings David and me closer together in unexpected ways, obliterates what came before. The more demands I learn to heed, the more competent I become at managing this messy, unwieldy contraption that is our family life—which works against all odds but which *works*—the more the past recedes. Soon I'll be a total amnesiac, second child or no.

One recent afternoon both Ben and Jean's daughter Emily fell asleep within minutes of each other during a stroll down Broadway. We stopped into a pastry shop for coffee but it reeked of leisure—of people who didn't have to measure time by length of nap, who weren't needed in a physical, immediate way. We ordered coffees to go and headed for the park to read the paper, watch the river. We rested for a while, and then we began to talk about our feelings toward our children. It was difficult. Our words sounded shallow, trite, awkward.

"Funny," Jean said. "It's so easy to talk about what's hard."

I was reminded of a conversation with a friend last summer during her week's visit to Hinsdale. She'd arrived with a suitcase full of books, needing to sit in the sun and bake a busted relationship out of her mind. Meanwhile, David and I ran after, sat with, read to, and cared for Benjamin. She envied us; we envied her.

One evening, after Ben had thrown a temper tantrum in the supermarket, she asked me how I did it. "You are infinitely patient, attentive, understanding . . . "

Well, temper tantrums or no, he was a wondrous child. Superstitiously I didn't want to elaborate too much, nor did I want to arouse her envy further. She had only to adjust her scale, look in the right places, and she'd see for herself all the plentiful evidence of his miraculous unfolding.

"I don't know," she said sadly, "that wouldn't be enough for me."

"But he's *mine,* he is me," I wanted to shout; "can't you see?" This is the real reason we can't talk about loving our kids to anyone else, even to Jean who wouldn't have been envious of or threatened by my disclosures. What restrains us is a sense of modesty. In a private moment we are free to acknowledge that our children are from us and of us. When I talk about loving Ben, I am talking about loving me, my husband, the sum of choices which is my life, our union. What he is, I am.

Sometimes I wish I didn't think that Ben was the best child in the world, the most beautiful, the smartest, the dearest. But I do. I don't act on this but keep it to myself, as does every other mother who thinks likewise about her child. Still, each time I study a picture of Ben with a young friend I think to myself: Imagine, that child's family is looking at the wrong baby.

But a part of me acknowledges that my friend had a point. Parenthood is fraught with sadness, tumult, poignancy. My children and I will fight, they'll despise things about me, they'll do their time on the couch. As David is fond of reminding me, at best we raise our children to be competent enough to leave us.

"When they sleep and their faces get flubby," Jean said after a long silence, "you can see how they'll look when they're older."

A second child? All I can say now is that I can't say for sure. Not soon, certainly. Maybe. I'm not saying no.

For a complete list of books available from
Penguin in the United States, write to Dept.
BA, Penguin Books, 299 Murray Hill Parkway,
East Rutherford, New Jersey 07073.

For a complete list of books available from
Penguin in Canada, write to Penguin Books
Canada Limited, 2801 John Street, Markham,
Ontario L3R 1B4.